THE LOVING SELF

BY

JOSEPH NATTERSON, M.D.

THE LOVING SELF

BY

JOSEPH NATTERSON, M.D.

IPBOOKS.net
International Psychoanalytic Books

International Psychoanalytic Books (IPBooks)
New York http://www.IPBooks.net

CONTENTS

PREFACE to Joseph Natterson's *The Loving Self*

By

David James Fisher

I remember attending a lecture in Paris by the Hegelian philosopher and 1960's guru, Herbert Marcuse. It left a major impression on me. He said expansively that a female student had recently asked him, "Professor Marcuse, what is love?" He replied that the question could not be answered in theory, but only in praxis.

Psychoanalytic practitioners know that the analytic situation is the best possible site for the emergence of love, for the study of all its ambiguities and uncertainties. Analysis creates the space both for the expression and empathic understanding of the fears and desires, the longings and vulnerabilities, connected to many varieties of love, including the love of children for parents, parents for children, sibling love, love of mentors, love of ideas, causes, social movements, and not least the multiple spectrum of romantic love. No better milieu exists, I believe, for the investigation of the practices of love, for the multiple ways individuals are derailed by love, fulfilled by love, are made crazy for and about love. Love is fundamental, essential, and life affirming; yet after over 125 years of clinical work and theorizing, we lack an adequate theory and explanation for how love works.

This is precisely the objective of Joseph Natterson's new and audacious book, *The Loving Self.* He provides a theory for the praxis of therapeutic love.

His book incorporates yet is critical toward many contributors to the psychoanalytic tradition. Natterson has had a long and distinguished career as a psychoanalyst. He has been practicing for over sixty years. He is the author of forty-two articles, book chapters, and book reviews, in addition to four books: *The Sexual Dream*, with Bernard Gordon (1977); *The Dream in Clinical Practice* (1980); *Beyond Countertransference* (1980); and *Primer of Intersubjectivity*, with Raymond Friedman, (1995).

In effect, Natterson's itinerary spans the period from psychoanalytic ego psychology, which he never fully embraced, to Alexander's "corrective emotional experience," to Kohut's self psychology, as he moved into the present with his own inquiry into the intersubjective aspects of the clinical context and contemporary relational theory. Natterson has long been recognized locally and nationally as a master clinician with an appreciation of the subtleties of the therapeutic process and the nuances of the analyst's subjectivity at play in this dialogue. He continues to have a busy practice and is held in high esteem for his teaching, remaining a popular supervisor—one with wit, wisdom, generosity of the spirit, and genuine caring for both supervisee and patient. I have often consulted with him to discuss cases, finding these conversations supportive, kind, and pregnant with ideas. He continues to demonstrate a powerful vitality and intellectual curiosity, including an ability to stay current with the contemporary literature in the field.

Natterson's book raises fundamental questions about what constitutes therapeutic action, about how change and cure emerge in the clinical context. Like most important books, this one has a thesis. Natterson argues that the liberation of the loving self ought to be the goal and outcome of any therapy, despite the presenting symptoms, regardless of the severity of the patient's psychopathology. He poetically sees the loving self as the "North Star" of psychotherapy, guiding, orienting, and buttressing the therapist against the uncertainties and regressive aspects of the work. Facilitating the emergence of the loving self is an emancipatory act, one that dissolves the feeling of futility and ineffectiveness that many therapists experience. To liberate the loving self in the patient is to provide an alternative to the anxious, guilt ridden, and inhibited self, a potent counter to the power self or false self that are grounded in fears and layers of self-protection and disavowal of affects.

In Natterson's technique, interpretation is critical to liberate the loving self. Interpretation vitalizes and deepens the intimacy of the therapeutic encounter. Interpretation ought to be grounded in the therapist's identification, empathy, and intuition. It is a manifestation of the therapist's love of the patient. It stems from the therapist's capacity for self-understanding and from his own ability to express his unconscious and preconscious understanding of how relationships unfold, develop, and mature. It presupposes a well-enough analyzed analyst. Interpretation is the method by which therapists relate, understand, and share themselves with their patients. It is a verbal way of communicating loving, nurturing, and sensitive feelings for the other. Natterson advocates a caring and attuned analytic attitude on the part of the therapist, one that pivots on kindness and intimacy, the receptive listening abilities of the therapist, and a comfortable identification with the patient's suffering and his potential to unlock and release his loving self. Removing the barriers to liberation will result in higher degrees of individuation, permitting the emergence of a psychosocial self that is engaged with one's community in a compassionate way. It also enhances the patient's ability to tolerate ambivalently held others.

Quoting Axel Honneth, Natterson beautifully states that love is "being oneself in another." Understanding oneself in a loving relationship requires not only sensitive attunement to the other, but also a sense of mutuality. He posits that the struggle for recognition is the root of love. Struggle of course implies conflict and conflict always suggests resistance and ambivalence. Authentic love cannot exist without self-respect and respect for the other; this is why narcissistic forms of love and defense are so defective in terms of releasing one's loving possibilities. Reification distorts, diminishes, and degrades the struggle for recognition. When a person is turned into a thing, or a part object, recognition is forgotten, or repressed. Therapy turning on the release of the loving self must be a form of "de-reification," a restoration of the desire for mutual recognition of the self and other. Love, Natterson contends, is always reciprocal.

The book includes many clinical vignettes illustrating his method of working to liberate the loving self. This sometimes requires him to find and liberate his loving feelings for the patient, which are not always easy to access. These clinical vignettes show Natterson at his best, where his practice illustrates his ideas, demonstrating how dramatic and even epiphanous moments occur in therapy. At these precious and moving moments, both participants experience exhilarating discoveries of the inner world and the space between two interacting subjectivities. The reader will encounter some fascinating characters like Mona, David, Riva, and Jill, while also observing how alive the clinical encounter can be. This is particularly true if the therapist is aware of and can monitor his subjective experiences. This gives the therapeutic encounter a realness and specificity that is often missing from other clinical reports. Natterson's self-revelations, disclosed to the reader and occasionally to the patient, and exploration of his subordinated and searching subjectivity, make these vignettes both entertaining to read and worthy of detailed study.

Let me conclude by acknowledging my respect and recognition of Natterson's contribution in this book. It will encourage the reader to think about, and possibly rethink, his or her own clinical assumptions. The book is a condensed summary statement based on decades of clinical immersion, deep reading and synthesis of the literature, and mature reflections on his life experience. He belongs to the romantic rather than the classical tradition in psychoanalysis. His concepts about the liberation of the loving self are strong, wise, and courageous, the fruits of an extended introspective process. The book is a short read, but a long think. It would be foolish, even cynical, to dismiss his ideas as idealistic or utopian, for much is at stake here. Natterson's book not only addresses the future emancipation of the individual from the prison house of his own inhibitions and impaired capacity to love, but also imagines the possibilities of a community and ultimately a planet that might be preserved and organized along more loving principles.

Foreword

"The Loving Self" has been a long-term project. I have brought together various interacting views of the human world and my life as a part of that world. My social, political, and religious attitudes have never been far from my therapeutic consciousness. In recent years, the idea of the loving self became my North Star, my intimate way of achieving a coherent synthesis of the existential forces that drive us, sometimes away from our highest potential. It is an idea that has proven to be useful, even critical, to my role as a therapist.

Presenting the loving self is my way of describing a person's complex psychosocial being. We are, after all, animals inhabiting a material world, who go on to create a cultural world. When we think of the loving self, we come to a better understanding of our true potential, of our sense of ourselves and of our relationship to each other and the world in which we live.

1.

Introduction

The world is undergoing an unprecedented environmental catastrophe. Mother Earth, who nurtures us all, urgently needs our utmost loving attention. Instead, we exploit and damage her ruthlessly, even as we claim to care deeply. The approach to therapy that I recommend awakens and restores the mature, humane capacities of individuals whose true, loving self has been stifled by impaired relational experiences. Once the loving self is awakened, a more loving stewardship of the planet will be possible.

I have been developing the concept of the Loving Self and its pertinence to psychotherapy for several years. But I am aware that the roots of this project lie deep within my personal history and my own self-development. I grew up in a family that professed and practiced humanistic, socially loving attitudes, but was, like all families, racked with ambivalence and its derivatives: fear, guilt, and inhibition. I always strove for a loving engagement with life, but I always stumbled on my own unconsciously created obstructions.

My decision to study and practice psychiatry and psychoanalysis arose from my wish to conquer fear. I now realize that, basically, I wished to release my loving self, although this fact was not clear to me for many years. From the outset of my career in psychotherapy, I intuitively declined the role of neutral, anonymous, and dispassionate observer. The term, "participant-observer" always seemed more apt, yet also incomplete. In 1991, I published *Beyond Countertransference*: *The Therapist's Subjectivity in the Therapeutic Process*. In that work, I, like others, insisted that therapeutic action arose basically from the interplay of deep forces in both patient and therapist.

Years later, *in Love and Psychotherapy*, I clearly stated that psychotherapy is a mutually loving process, through which arises a concurrent unfolding of self, in both parties. It took only a short conceptual step further for me to realize that this mature self, having arisen from loving interaction, is indeed a loving self. I began to focus on the loving self in my practice of psychoanalytic therapy, in my supervision, and in my formal teaching.

Recently, two books have appeared that I regard as highly supportive of the substantial validity of the loving self. *On Kindness*, by Adam Phillips and Barbara Taylor, argues that we humans are hardwired to be kind and that genuine kindness is indispensable for relational happiness and social well-being. Phillips and Taylor propose a "kindness instinct" as the source of this universal human potential for kindness. But they recognize the deep ambivalence that each individual must encounter and resolve in himself in order that genuine kindness may govern our intimate and social relations.

In Jeremy Rifkin's work, *The Empathic Civilization*, the author provides a convergent concept. He proposes that cultural progress, even survival, demand a massive proliferation of empathy. Empathic potentials exist in individuals and in groups. These need to be identified and fostered. Then the forces of empathy may defeat the process of entropy and ultimately, self-destruction. By destroying the planet, we destroy our ability to survive.

The works of Rifkin and of Phillips and Taylor are excellent examples of current sociopolitical and psychological thought into which the concept of the loving self fits quite comfortably and appropriately. This book offers an approach to psychotherapy, one that focuses on the loving self.

Patients come to therapists with a wide spectrum of complaints that range from agoraphobia to zoophobia, and include such diverse problems as anxiety, discontent with a job, family dysfunction, insomnia, irritable bowel, unhappy marriage—the list is endless. Even though one individual's complaint is psychophysiological and another's is a troubled relationship, the unifying objective remains the liberation of the loving self and the realization of an inner state of freedom and safety in which it can thrive. While each therapeutic relationship or dialogue is utterly unique, the loving self can be the North Star that guides every therapeutic journey.

Sometimes this journey can seem overwhelming, even futile, at the outset. But when the therapist realizes that the unfolding of the loving self is the central axis of the therapeutic experience, she can immerse herself in the specific urgent manifestations of the patient. The underlying malfunctioning of the patient's loving self and its consequent role in the patient's problems become a clear priority; feelings of futility and ineffectiveness dissolve.

Individuals who experienced nurturance, care, and love in infancy and childhood are endowed with a viable loving self. Yet, in such persons, the neurotic impositions by parents who love their child ambivalently result in the inhibitions and malfunctioning that produce the rich tapestry of complaints that patients bring to the therapist. The initial exploration of the patient's important narrative and relational themes helps show how these themes participate in suppressing the loving self. That is the first step.

The Unfolding

When the loving self emerges from hiding, the patient's loving capabilities are always enhanced. Self and love are inseparable partners, wrapped around each other like a double helix. Love moves from the longing to be loved, to the belief that one is worthy of being loved, to the confident certainty that one has or will have love. Parallel to this, the self unfolds, moving from self-doubt to self-trust, self-respect, and self-esteem.

Quite remarkably, this perspective reveals multiple exploratory pathways, which lead to important discoveries. It is as though the invocation of the loving self in therapy stimulates exciting questions about present and past relations to others and to oneself. This, in turn, can replace what might have been, in both parties, a dispiriting sense of disabling uncertainty in the therapeutic process with a constructive attitude of steady dialogic advance and a new clarity of understanding that is neither false nor misleading. Its source is the deep intuition that originates with the struggle in every person to discover and liberate the loving self.

Interpretation is central to the release of the loving self. To interpret is to relate, understand, share oneself with the other. It is a vital, pulsating component of caring, i.e., loving. The interpretive emphasis on the loving self and the defenses that inhibit it is itself a loving stance. Interpretation vitalizes and enhances intimacy. It expedites the emergence of the loving self. Surprisingly, it also renders the endless complexity of an individual's psychological world more evident. It provides a guiding principle. As the individual's loving self gains ascendancy, an open appreciation of this boundless complexity enables a fruitful exploration.

Each person develops his new and unique experience of love. The endless variations of human individuation constantly present a stimulating challenge to the contemporary therapist. It is my recommendation that the therapist seek and foster the loving self at all times, whether it seems absent or is clearly manifest. The variety of false self-defenses, which coalesce around issues of power, such as domination, sadism, submission, compliance, appeasement, masochism, and other non-loving features, show both the complexity and the promise of this work in its approach to removing the barriers to the liberation of the loving self.

Paradoxically, this simplification of the theoretical approach actually enables the therapist to perceive and intervene with greater subtlety than would be possible if she did not have the loving self in mind. It does not reduce the rich complexity of the process to a simplistic clarity or order, but rather adds sensitivity, strength, and resourcefulness to the therapeutic instrument.

The concept of the Loving Self complements and is a natural evolution of the indispensable ideas in psychoanalytic therapy that have been generated since Freud. It has grown out of all that hard and heroic effort by many workers. This book names the loving self, emphasizes the interpenetration of love and self, and asserts the basic role of love in the therapeutic process.

2.

Love in Psychotherapy

Psychotherapy is fundamentally a loving process. In the past it was believed that love was either an accomplishment of therapy (the patient learned how to love) or a problem that arose during the course of treatment (inappropriately erotic attitudes developed between patient and therapist that obstructed therapy). Now we can acknowledge that love is a fundamental, creative, and propulsive force in therapy, and that therapy is a mutually loving process that invariably involves the subordinated subjectivity of the therapist. We may now also assume that most patients bring developed but inhibited loving capabilities to therapy. These inhibitions originate from strictures imposed by loving but neurotic parents. Therapy logically becomes a process of removing these inhibitions and releasing the loving self. From this it follows that love and self are inseparable and mutually reinforcing, and that the authentic self is the loving self.

Jonathan Lear wrote on this subject, "Psychoanalysis, Freud once said, is a cure through love." He added, "But the latent content of this remark, which Freud only gradually discovered, and then through a glass darkly, is that psychoanalysis promoted individuation. In that sense, psychoanalysis is itself a manifestation of love. And the emergence of psychoanalysis on the human scene must, from this perspective, be part of love's developmental history." Furthermore, Lear noted, "The individual is in his essence, a response to love: it is from the internalization of love that an I is constituted."

Liberating the Loving Self

Love is relational and inter-subjective. It is a relationship of mutual recognition in which each person values the uniqueness of the other, while also finding oneself in the other and appreciating the profound interdependence that connects the two. Gaylin wrote, "When properly understood, love and need to be loved will be seen as more powerful motivating forces in human behavior than the desire for sexual release," and, "…by modifying the sense of self it allows unselfish behavior to serve self-interest."

The notion that an individual is a completely separate being is an illusion. Human being and human subjectivity are seamless and collectively interdependent and interpenetrating. Honneth reminds us that two hundred years ago, Hegel emphasized how, in loving one another, we realize the concrete nature of our own needs and accept each other as needy beings. It is this acknowledgment of our essential interdependence that unites us.

Love is also an evolving social phenomenon. Within the vast, inter-subjective social cosmos, the loving self forms in a social as well as individual context. We are fortunate that one important postmodern trend, among many disparate ones, is the recognition that loving social processes are a basic human necessity. To grow up in a society that promotes loving and non-exploitive relations among groups and individuals is to enjoy an environment that facilitates development of the loving self. (This would be Rifkin's empathic environment.)

Bourdieu, citing Merleau-Ponty, says the individual knows the world "without objectifying distance, takes it for granted, precisely because he is caught up in it, bound up with it: he inhabits it like a garment [*un habit*] or a familiar habitat. He feels at home in the world because the world is also in him, in the form of *habitus*, a virtue made of necessity, which implies a form of love of necessity, *amor fati*." We are of the world: it is in us, and we are in it. Clearly, the loving self is a psychosocial self. My version of this basic assumption goes as follows: the self is made up of an individual's crucial developmental relationships. So the significant relational others (mother, father, siblings) live on as ineradicable and indispensable elements of the self. Of this we have no choice; we are these others, warts and all. Until we realize and welcome these ambivalently held others, through whom we learned love and hate, we remain unemancipated, and our unique individuality remains relatively stifled.

How does this idea apply to the therapeutic process? Simply put, when the patient and therapist engage one another, an important relational issue is relived and therefore subject to transformation, hence to liberation and enlargement of the self.

Obviously, the patient is not a child to the therapist, nor is the therapist a parent to the patient. Yet a symbiotic arc does exist between their shared experience of dependency and individuation in a context of mutual caring. Inevitably, the patient's deep, family-based relationships are relived in the therapeutic relationship. The provision of care tends to be more ample from the therapist, and the dependency/individuation needs are preponderant in the patient. This asymmetric but reciprocal process of mutual care is basic to love and to psychotherapy.

Over a century ago, Freud's free-associative and interpretive approach hinted at the underlying inter-subjective/relational essence of therapy. Further analytic landmarks include Ferenczi's concept of mutual analysis (1932), Alexander and French's formulation of the corrective emotional experience (1946), Reik's emphasis on analysis as a duet (1948), Greenson's introduction of the working alliance (1965), Racker's inter-subjective version of Kleinian analysis (1968), and Kohut's appreciation of the crucial necessity for the analyst's empathic responsiveness (1977). These pioneering contributions led to psychotherapy's current flowering of inter-subjective/relational understanding.

Therapy's basic process is not to fill vacancies, but to liberate what has been kept hidden, which is, first and foremost, the loving self. Therapists sometimes see cases in which a patient's fluent loving capability emerges and prevails within a relatively short period of time. Such events suggest that the loving self had survived intact from early childhood, but had been inhibited and stifled. This contradicts a commonly held notion that the patient comes to therapy with a deficient self, which the therapist fills by providing a previously missing loving object.

But when rapid gains toward achieving a loving life occur, it seems fair to assume that a solid loving self has always been present, having been generated in infancy and childhood. While neurotically dysfunctional families can frequently provide a sufficiently loving experience, the child's loving self will often suffer hindrance and suppression from the parents' neurotic impositions. Therapy's task is to gain access to the patient's powerful loving potential, which has been masked and subjugated by anxiety that developed in the child in its dealings with the loving but neurotic parents. The actualization of the patient's fundamental loving aspect occurs through the mutually caring nature of the therapeutic experience.

The Emancipating Journey

The emancipating journey begins at the outset of therapy. The patient comes to the therapist initially to be helped with a particular problem. Implicit here is the desire for recognition in the framework of a relationship, because the patient anticipates understanding and empathy through the therapist's caring interest. Initially, the therapist's conscious intent is to help the patient through psychological understanding; but what else is this effort than a desire to recognize and affirm the patient's subjectivity?

The therapeutic relationship begins as the inter-subjective dialogue opens. It gradually or quickly becomes a loving one as the dialogue implicitly revolves around the role of love in the patient's life. Furthermore, psychotherapy in our era tends to focus on the enhancement of self. The achievement of a powerful loving experience correlates regularly with a more complete unfolding of self. Again, love and self connect with one another like a double helix. And since the aim of therapy is now the strengthening of self, the experience of love correspondingly increases. As this can only happen in a situation of reciprocity, fostering a patient's loving potentials occurs only in a mutually loving relationship.

The tactful and timely interpretations and advice that arise from the therapist's silent empathic formulations of issues are expressions of love for the patient. Other kinds of feelings also arise between therapist and patient, including envy, hate, distrust, and contempt. Kohut suggests that such negating sentiments reveal a disturbance of self. I emphasize that these aspects of therapeutic struggle recapitulate issues that originated in early development. They arise during therapy as an unavoidable manifestation of the effort exerted by both parties to arrive at a loving relationship and achieve a fully actualized self.

Fluency and the Loving Self

Fluent interpretations by the therapist are expressions of love, even though the recipient may sometimes have difficulty accepting them. But such interpretations are not a one-sided bestowal of love, because, from the beginning, the therapist is receiving and responding to hints of love from the patient. These are detectable, even when the subject appears on the surface to be averse or immune to entering into a loving relationship with the therapist.

Optimally, therapists are aware that the actualization of love is a foremost goal of therapy, and is inseparable from the liberation of self. The sustained appreciation of the loving imperative enables the therapist to formulate precise interpretations that intensify the therapeutic process. Where my own patients are concerned, I try to maintain a continuous background consciousness of the role of love in my therapeutic work, even when the patient and I are discussing other important matters. In this way, coherent and pertinent interpretations of the core problem of love can be more readily developed, thus facilitating optimal actualization of the loving self. For example, a person may come to therapy initially over a very disturbed relationship with much bitterness and/or guilt. From the outset, I ponder the real possibility that the sound and fury may be concealing intense but inhibited underlying love.

Subordinated Subjectivity and Searching Subjectivity

Let's consider the loving therapeutic interaction. In the therapeutic dyad, of course the two persons are taking different roles, one as therapist and one as patient. But another distinctive asymmetry is also present: In therapy the therapist's subjectivity is always active, along with the patient's. However, an important difference is in play as well. The therapist, due to greater experience and self- knowledge, is able to achieve a *subordinated subjectivity*, which, in turn, becomes *searching subjectivity*. As a therapist, subordinated and searching subjectivity are crucial to my attunement, to my interpretive readiness, and to my identificatory sensitivity.

To understand this asymmetry, we need to examine the characteristics of the underlying inter-subjective process. It is assumed that the basic "structure" of the self consists of the active assemblage of the individual's basic lived (and living) developmental relationships. We may call these relational (or narrative) themes. The fulfilling (or unfulfilling) quality of these relational themes determines the degree to which the individual has achieved actualization of the loving self. In other words, each has the potential to act as a stumbling block to the emergence of the loving self. So, in optimal therapeutic process, the pertinent relational theme of the patient interacts in a bilaterally mutative way with the corresponding relational theme of the therapist.

The therapist may or may not be conscious of this underlying thematic interaction, but it is a *sine qua non* of therapy. Its success depends on the suitably subordinated subjectivity of the therapist. Not so for the patient, whose subjective experience will be initially untamed and in the grip of relational distortions. Relatively, the therapist will be more aware of her own relational issues and conflicts, less anxious or otherwise disturbed by their interactive emergence. This sophisticated acceptance of self, on the part of the therapist, enables an empathic attitude, receptive listening, and more comfortable identification with the patient, as well as more creative interpretation. We see here the loving self of the therapist facilitating the actualization of the patient's loving self.

We might profitably conceive of the self as follows: the self has structure and function. Structure may be seen basically as the relatively stable interaction of the intricately engaged relational themes occurring within the self. The functions of the self may be defined as identification and interpretation. As noted elsewhere, the two parties of the therapeutic dyad are continuously identifying with and interpreting other and self. This process of loving interaction steadily enlarges the loving self of both parties.

3.

Theorists of Love: Progenitors of the Loving Self

Hegel, early in the nineteenth century, asserted, "Recognition is man." He was proposing that the *struggle for recognition* is the most powerful underlying motivating force of human psychological and cultural development.

Honneth paraphrased Hegel as follows:

"Love represents the first stage of reciprocal recognition because, in it, subjects mutually confirm each other with regard to the concrete nature of their needs, and thereby recognize each other as needy creatures. In the reciprocal experience of loving, both subjects know themselves to be united in their neediness, in their dependence on each other. (Honneth, 1996, p.95)

In the same article, Honneth reasserts Hegel's view that love is "being oneself in another," and that attainment of love is the first step in the universal struggle for recognition.

According to Winnicott's persuasive ideas, the loving process originates with the state of fusion, un-differentiation, and primary inter-subjectivity in which the infant and mother exist. Winnicott (1969) helped establish the struggle for recognition as the root of love and the loving self through his concept of the good enough mother. He proposed that after the earliest mother-infant symbiosis, the mother becomes able to engage with the child in its need to individualize against the all-enveloping mother-infant inter-relationship. He summarizes this process as follows:

"1). Subject relates to object. 2). Object is in process of being found instead of being placed by subject in the world. 3). Subject destroys object.

4). Object survives destruction. 5). Subject can use object." (1965, p.94)

In other words, we may say: 1) Infant and mother first exist in a state of fusion, of primary inter-subjectivity. 2) Infant begins to recognize the real mother out there instead of relating only to a mother who is undifferentiated from the infant. 3) The infant has to attack and destroy this illusory mother in order to find the real mother out there. 4) If the mother is good enough to absorb this destruction without retaliation, she will have survived the attack and become a real person for the child. 5) Now the child can recognize and love the real mother out there.

The mother is not simply facilitating the infant's recognition of her as a separate psychological being, she is also growing and enjoying a parallel appreciation of the child's increasingly differentiated and complex subjective life. As she both resists and encourages the child's individuation, she recognizes herself in the child as well as the child in herself. The nucleus of the child's loving self is formed out of this conflict.

In the mid-twentieth century, Hans Loewald stated that, in analysis, "We encounter and make use of what is known under the general title of: identification. The patient and the analyst identify to an increasing degree, if the analysis proceeds, in their ego activity of scientifically guided self-scrutiny."

I believe that, in our current inter-subjective language, he is saying that reciprocal identification between patient and therapist is essential for therapeutic action to occur, and that the therapeutic relationship arises from this core identification of therapist and patient.

Further, Loewald insisted that the therapist maintain "…focus on the patient's emerging core, requiring […] an objectivity and neutrality, the essence of which is love and respect for the individual and individual development." Here, Loewald infused the traditional terms, objectivity and neutrality, with a paradoxical meaning, namely love and respect. Thus, objectivity and neutrality dissolve into subjectivity. The objective, neutral therapist becomes a fictive assumption, replaced by an identifying, loving therapist.

Since the self in therapy develops through love and respect, we may now assume that the self is a loving self, at core, having flourished on a diet of abundant love from the caring other.

In the same essay, Loewald asserted, "The analyst in his interpretations reorganizes, reintegrates unconscious material for himself as well as for the patient, since he has to be attuned to the patient's unconscious, using, as we say, his own unconscious as a tool in order to arrive at the organizing interpretation." Clearly, this means the therapist is interpreting and changing himself as well as the patient. Reciprocal interpretation is inseparable from reciprocal identification. So the self, bred in love, inevitably is a loving self, an identifying and interpreting self.

Now, here is what I call "Honneth's triad." In the early days of America, in the "Little Red Schoolhouse," children learned the three R's: Readin', Ritin', Rithmetic. Honneth has given us a new three R's: Recognition, Respect, and Reification.

Axel Honneth is a distinguished German moral philosopher and social theorist. His interest in psychoanalysis—particularly the work of Loewald and Winnicott—enables him to enlarge our understanding of the postmodern psychoanalytic self. While his triad of recognition, respect, and reification has societal implications extending far beyond the psychoanalytic self, his three R's reveal illuminating dimensions of the postmodern loving self.

Recalling Hegel's terse insistence that "Recognition is man," we can readily appreciate that the *struggle for recognition* constitutes the fundamental process through which individual and socio-cultural evolution unfolds. This position from Hegel, elaborated by Honneth, also emphasizes the related basic role of love as utterly coextant with the struggle for recognition. Honneth vigorously contests Machiavelli's and Hobbes' insistence that man is a ferociously and selfishly competitive creature, "bloody in tooth and nail," in need of a sovereign of absolute power, ruling by divine right, who must contain man's base nature in order to achieve some degree of social civility.

Recognition of the other as a sentient, needy creature is inseparable from the need to perceive that the other sees one similarly—seeing oneself in the other, and vice-versa: separateness while experiencing sameness. These events are basic to the formation of the self. Honneth states that the first step in the struggle for recognition is this interactive achievement of love in the intimate mother-child relationship, which, in turn, breeds *self-confidence*.

In 1992, Jessica Benjamin wrote:

It is certainly true that recognition begins with the other's confirming response that tells us we have created meanings, had an impact, revealed an intention. But very early on we begin to find that recognition between persons—understanding and being understood, being in attunement—begins to be an end in itself. Recognition between persons is essentially mutual. By our very enjoyment of the other's confirming response, we recognized her in return. (p.47)

The Citizen-Self and Solidarity

Respect, the goal of the second phase of the struggle for recognition, has a broad socio-political reach, but remains vital in the striving for selfhood. A few of the important landmarks in the struggle for respect are Magna Carta, the Reformation, the ideas of Descartes, the French Revolution, and the American Civil War. These shared a common purpose: reducing or abolishing the power of a monarch or privileged group to deprive another part of the population of its *legal personhood*. When slaves become freemen, when subjects become citizens, this new codified social status enormously enhances the self-respect of the emancipated population. Self-love and social love both gain. Self-respect, enjoyed by the individual, strengthens loving social bonds. And so, establishment of rights is indispensable. Rights express the individual's self-respectful belief in entitlement. This belief arises in part from societal policies and practices that articulate and reinforce individual rights. Psychotherapy emphasizes the inner achievement of self-respect, hence establishing a predisposition to the claiming of rights.

To illustrate the importance of "rights" in the optimal unfolding and function of the loving self, here is a brief, unsolicited letter from a middle-aged woman, two years after successful completion of her therapy:

I've been giving a little thought to our work together. What comes most to mind is how I used up every bitter detail I could dredge up about my father and how you took it all in and honored it in that special way you have of taking in and honoring. When I was left with nothing else to talk about except my despair about the continuing strained mistrust, sadness, even dislike, I felt towards him, I remember so clearly your forthright remark: 'You have a right to have a loving relationship with your father.' After everything I'd said about him, you defined my plight in a way I'd never understood before—that is, that I had a "right." Also, I'd never thought of having a "loving relationship" with my father. I'd been merely striving for a tolerable relationship. You made it possible for me to express my tolerance as love, which, I realized almost at once, came much more fluently and naturally to me. Gradually, the manifestation of my more loving nature had a positive effect upon him. He became more open and gracious and loving toward me; and everything blossomed from there.

Self-esteem, Honneth says, is not achieved solely by having self-confidence, rights, and self-respect. The additional requirement is that individuals be valued by their fellow human beings for their contribution to the community. This phenomenon is called solidarity.

Reclaiming the Loving Self

Reification is Honneth's third R. In Latin, Res means "thing." In Honneth's usage, reification means turning a person into a thing. More precisely, he calls it "the forgetfulness of recognition." Honneth has said that the impetus for his interest in reification was his horrified incomprehension of how young German soldiers in WWII could shoot Jewish mothers and babies in the back of the head without guilt, shame, or remorse.

Reification and recognition are totally incompatible. Since love arises through the relational struggle for recognition, it is evident that as reification increases, there is a proportionate reduction in the experiencing of love—probably in the scope of one's loving interest and in the quality of one's most intimate loving experience.

Honneth's "forgetfulness of recognition" obviously indicates that reification is a product of decay. The proto-loving human bonding has been erased, i.e., forgotten, and an inevitable objectifying dehumanization of the other replaces it. Critics such as Judith Butler and Jonathan Lear challenge Honneth and accuse him of oversimplifying the problem of alienation in contemporary life by committing a sentimental pre-lapserian fallacy. But this becomes a debate beyond the scope of this book.

Honneth's emphasis on forgetfulness of recognition invites us to retrieve the forgotten; to restore memory. What could be more compatible with a psychoanalytic orientation? And in therapy, the most beneficial change is in the patient's loving experience of his or her world. For me, Honneth's allegedly wishful fallacy provides a conceptual undergirding for the clinical notion of a repressed or dissociated loving self, a loving self that has been forgotten or mislaid in a clinical manifestation of reification. Therefore, therapy might be defined as a process of de-reification.

4.

Identification, Interpretation, and the Loving Self

Humanity's need for empathic, kind, and loving communal life is urgent. The loving self is the optimal condition of self for our era. Since public life and individual life are continuous, a loving self is all the more proper and fitting. I have mentioned the work of Jeremy Rifkin, Adam Phillips, and Barbara Taylor. But it is by no means an entirely new idea, if you recall Freud's classic remark that the goal of psychotherapy is to love and to work. From its very beginning, psychoanalysis was a way to uncover the loving self, and by extension, a more empathic communal life.

The loving self loves itself, loves other(s), and is loved by other(s). The potential for this optimal state exists in most patients. Why? Because a deep, loving experience with parents occurs at the earliest time in most peoples' lives, only to become obstructed and inhibited by the neurotic impositions of the parents in the course of family life. Thus, paradoxically, the very parents who were indispensable to the creation of the loving self later force it into hiding.

The therapeutic process liberates the potential loving self through reciprocal and loving interaction between therapist and patient. Therapists, in their pursuit of this goal, can regard the loving self as the North Star guiding their journey. Let me emphasize here that this focus is quite compatible with therapist openness, restraint, receptiveness, and non-intrusive associative listening. In fact, it is my impression that this orientation enhances therapeutic discipline and suppleness.

Unless a self interprets, it cannot identify; unless a self identifies, it cannot interpret. Interpretation and identification are inseparably glued together, indispensable to one another and yet not identical—neither one precedes or supersedes the other. We might consider that the basic functions of the self consist in just these two elements—identification and interpretation.

Identification depends on feeling and intuition, whereas interpretation depends on thinking and analysis. It's important to realize, however, that thought and feeling are only different angles of relating. They are not categorically distinct. If I identify with someone, I feel with and for him. I feel like him. This simple event diminishes the potential objectification of the other person and stimulates my thinking about him, which in turn elaborates and amplifies my love for him. This, of course, is inter-subjective and presupposes that he is also lovingly feeling for and thinking about me. Otherwise, the loving symbiotic arc cannot sustain itself, and each party withdraws as bilateral objectification supervenes.

The Ultimate Two-Way Street

The therapist identifies with the patient and interprets the patient. The two processes are different but inseparable, and they go on simultaneously. When I am with a patient, I listen with feeling, and I do believe that our feelings are shared. This is a different kind of feeling—perhaps we can say that it is listening with poignancy rather than pleasure or pain; I give myself over to the other without sacrificing my separateness. This occurs when I am functioning with *subordinated subjectivity*, without which the patient's path to a more loving self is narrower and more obstructed.

For example, the patient reveals a secret that is guilt-laden—selfish, destructive, etc. This mobilizes a memory in me of one of my similar transgressions. I feel suitably miserable, but the reaction is subdued. I am also thinking about how my painful memory may provide understanding of the patient's similarly painful issue (and this questioning by me is an aspect of interpretation—since I am thinking about meaning).

The therapist gives herself over to the patient, yet the therapist is not abandoning self. So here we have the therapist who strives to feel with the other person and disdains any trace of a holier-than-thou attitude, but at the same time, while becoming the patient, the therapist retains a separate concept of self. In this way, the therapist provides a living example of how a loving self might handle and utilize painful memories.

Likeness prevails, but separateness maintains itself, and thereby the therapist can function as a loving critic—of the patient and oneself. This loving critic may actually be the optimal interpreter: feeling identified with the patient, viewing the shared sinfulness as miscarried loving effort, realizing its unconscious derivation, and then experiencing self-acceptance rather than self-reproach. In this way, other people in the patient's life can be similarly perceived as pursuing loving goals in ineffective ways—rather than misperceived with hostile interpretations.

Letting oneself identify with the patient (become the patient) opens the portals of lovingly critical thought. This almost instantaneous process—finding the other through oneself—means bilateral maturation rather than one-sidedness (judgment and forgiveness).

We can assume that the loving self is a thinking self. The loving self cares about the well-being and fulfillment of the loved other—*it is thoughtful* in the truest sense of the word. Thoughts occur as integral parts of the inter-subjective relationship. In other words, in a loving relationship, the relationship stimulates gently speculative reflection in both parties about the ongoing subjective experience of both. So we may confidently assume that the loving self is a continuously interpreting self and that this thinking about self and other is fundamental to a loving relationship. I suggest that love is always reciprocal, and in this loving condition, creative interactional thinking about subjective relational meaning occurs.

But what about "love" that is not reciprocal? If, for example, the desire for another person is repudiated or exploited, rather than shared, then this yearning is not love. Probably such unilateral infatuation or fascination with another person should be regarded as fetishism. It is not mutual, therefore not inter-subjective, hence not love.

From an inter-subjective standpoint such a fetishistic experience might usefully be viewed as a perversion of love, resulting from an underlying unconscious narrative theme that precludes fulfillment in love. An unconsciously based prohibition of loving and being loved results in a compulsion to focus desire on an unaccepting other.

Interpretive Thought in the Material World

In "Truth and Method" Gadamer distinguished between two basically different kinds of thinking. One kind is scientific thought. It is methodical, systematic, aimed toward describing and understanding the material domains of science. However, these are not the domains of the loving self. Gadamer proposes interpretive thought as quite different from scientific thought, which tries to explain the facts of the material world. Instead, interpretive thought seeks (and creates) human meaning. It is inseparable from human subjectivity, and indispensable for the loving self. The loving self exists in the sphere of relationships, self-understanding, understanding of others, morality, ethics, aesthetics, and creative self-expression. This, then, is the sphere of interpretive thought.

Love and Language

The most elemental relational understanding is probably preverbal, or nonverbal. But language is deeply involved—and ultimately crucial—in richly elaborated loving understanding. Gadamer's dramatic assertion, "Being that can be understood is language," captures the necessity of language for fully developed, loving, interpretive relational experience. Gadamer explains that language is much more than a stock of words, a vocabulary, a structure of grammar and syntax. He asserts that every word, uttered or thought, resonates with the entire universe of human consciousness.

One might propose that rudimentary love can exist without language, but language cannot exist without love. As the individual develops, mature love is crucially dependent upon language. The loving self requires language in order to thrive. The optimal clarification and conveyance of interpretive thought in relationship requires language; hence the loving, interpretive self is also a linguistic self.

Honneth asserts that cognition, rational thinking, cannot occur without the prior relational engagement of the person. The young child must first experience a sense of coherent human relatedness, and can then proceed to reliable, rational thought. The relational precursor is essential. From all this we can be certain that the loving self is a thinking, verbal, and interpreting self. We can appreciate that the loving self is a thoughtful self, caringly thoughtful about the other. Love and thought are inseparable.

Subordinated Subjectivity At Work

A middle-aged man came for therapy because, in the previous months, he had begun to have cascading fears of driving—especially dread that he would run a stop sign or a traffic signal and thereby cause a terrible accident. So, getting into the drivers' seat became a nightmare. Secondarily, he had become depressed, withdrawn, and unproductive. Medication and reassurance by his internist provided little help, and so, urged by his wife, he sought therapy.

During the very early visits with me, the patient unloaded his painful story—graphically, vividly, and appallingly. Especially noteworthy was his repeated statement that he was always an anxious child who longed for encouragement from his father, a busy professional who seemed unavailable to the patient. Something was very much needed from the father, but it was missing.

In every way, Edward exuded a strident need for me to relieve and protect him. This attitude invited an exceptional thoughtfulness from me. I responded to his intense implicit expectation of help from me with the activation of a deep rescue fantasy, part of my complicated developmental history as the youngest in a large family world of thwartedness.

Importantly, Edward informed me that severe anxiety began soon after an important script that he had submitted to a director was mercilessly criticized and rejected by the director. His initial feelings of hurt and inadequacy rapidly changed into his anxiety symptoms. The reactive anger was only barely conscious.

The intensity of my empathic response encouraged me to offer to him, as early as the third session, this powerfully charged interpretation: He experienced the script rejection as a punitive dismissal by an aloof father figure and this, in turn, released deeply embedded unconscious guilt, which, as it moved toward consciousness, generated severe anxiety that his incompetence would cause a street disaster.

He immediately responded with feelings of being understood, recognized, loved. And he then reported that he had perceived marginal anger when the script was rejected, but these feelings were largely submerged by the massive loss of self confidence and self esteem that led into his anxiety state.

Edward now felt safe with me, feeling unconditional acceptance, and this led to a surprising disclosure: He told me that he had suffered with severe and intermittent obsessive anxiety since early adolescence—an unshakeable belief that he was infected with a venereal disease and that in sexual intimacy he would infect his partner. So in all his premarital relations and in his marital relations he feared he could transmit the disease to his partner. Of course, in all his physical examinations, no evidence of such disease was ever found. He had never, ever, shared this fear-belief with anyone until, in the relieving ambience of our reciprocally loving dialogue, he made this salvational revelation.   Furthermore,   this obsessive fear first emerged in the following manner. From the dawn of consciousness, sexual feelings and thoughts had always been fascinating and guilt-soaked. Then, in puberty, he had initiated sexual activity with two boys, and he suffered intense guilt over these actions. These events precipitated his delusion that he was carrying a sexually transmitted disease.

As these important memories and connections poured out, he began to remember that, at around age five or six years, he had been seduced sexually by an adult male family friend. Recovery of this memory and its attendant painful emotions led directly to a realization of the underlying true meaning of his sexual misadventures. Namely, throughout his childhood, and into his adult life, he yearned in pain for a warm, protective response from his father.

In his experience with me, Edward felt safe and loved, as by a loving father. All this activated spontaneity in him. He did not confess his sinful memories to me, rather, he shared them lovingly with me. My own counterpart paternal narrative theme involving feelings of insufficient fathering enabled me to identify with Edward's suffering, and this loving identification facilitated the therapeutic dialogue.

Edward's anxiety melted away, and his chronic false belief that he was infected and dangerous disappeared. All this benefit occurred rapidly— during the early months of therapy.

The rapidity with which beneficial change occurred was based on the productive interaction of our respective loving selves. Even in his initial misery, I sensed that his loving capabilities were not deeply buried and would become evident in response to my rapid interpretive reach into the salient developmental issues mentioned above. He was primed to think in a lovingly ambivalent way about the influential role of important past experience in his present relational life.

This therapeutic collaboration developed quite rapidly due to his readiness to form a loving alliance between us. It was as though a veneer of symptomatic resistance in him was covering a strongly loving self, pressing for freedom. I was prepared to identify with him through my subordinated subjectivity. We embraced interpretively through the porous barrier. Out of this commingling of resonant thoughts, his loving self was reborn.

Searching Subjectivity and Epiphany

Interpretation, while distinct, is not separable from the inter-subjective experience itself. A searching subjectivity seeks out the yearning subjectivity of the other. It is interpreting as it engages. And since interpretation becomes reflective thought, we can say that reflection is already beginning with the initial experience. Even in infancy, as the innocent, naïve, inter-subjective process occurs, proto-reflection and proto-interpretation may be occurring. An interpreting dialogue is optimal for psychotherapy. Following unconscious and conscious subjective experience, the therapist is silently interpreting self, while audibly, but judiciously, interpreting the self of the other.

In the course of extended, exploratory psychotherapy, an epiphanic moment often takes place, in which an exhilarating discovery of the world occurs. This event is a new birth of the loving self, now able to leave the stultifying safety of the neurotic womb. The inner world and the outer world become beautiful. Awareness of continuing problems is even more clear than before, but mastery is achieved and action is taken. An attitude of informed and hopeful confidence drives away the depressing obsessing that had passively prevailed.

The epiphany expresses the culmination of major changes that had been occurring below the surface of conscious dialogue, involving inter-subjective interpretive intimacy. The accumulating benefits of psychotherapy regularly become evident to one or both participants in the therapeutic experience, even without the epiphanic event. Yet the beauty of the epiphany lies in its role as a confirming seal of liberation of the long-suffering, stifled self that no longer must rely on false self-adaptation.

In contemporary psychotherapy, epiphanies have a special function. They demonstrate the overflowing effects of the now freed loving self. This thrilling experience arises neither from pharmacological intervention nor from behavioral modification. It occurs only with the massive rush to freedom of the loving self.

At its core, the therapeutic process consists in the merging of a relational theme of the patient with a matching theme of the therapist. The effective therapist identifies continuously with the patient. The intensity of this identification fluctuates, as does the therapist's awareness of the identification. But the therapist's identification is indispensable. The therapist must constantly be able to put himself in the patient's place, thus becoming the patient while also remaining separate and different. This is part of what I term the therapist's "subordinated subjectivity." And this identification is also inseparable from interpretation, which arises naturally in the process.

Self-Absorbed and Other-Absorbed

During therapy, the patient is appropriately self-absorbed, while the therapist is intentionally other-absorbed (as well as self-absorbed). This dual absorption of the therapist becomes possible because he has a well-established familiarity with his inner world and is relatively comfortable with its events. Over the years, the therapist steadily refines his understanding of his relational themes and their role in his relational life. Those life issues remaining problematic for the therapist will create surplus anxiety and will thus diminish fluent deployment of his subjectivity for identification and interpretation.

Work on himself is therefore an endless obligation for the therapist. Such conscientious effort reduces shocks, jarring surprises, and other unbearable affective states. Instead, the inter-subjectively mature and informed therapist enjoys suitably attenuated emotional reactions, and understands the relational issues of which they are a part. In this way, the therapist generates cogent interpretations that meet the patient's need, thereby enlarging the range of the loving self.

The optimal therapist is in touch with his own life theme and its poignancy, while also feeling the patient's related experience. This identification occurs because the therapist's subjectivity is scanning the horizon of subjectivity and is drawn to the patient's own subjective zone of turbulence.

Any resistance to his own inner life and his loving self reduces the therapist's capacity to identify with the patient. In turn, the patient's troubling relational theme cannot reach accessible horizonal position and form, and the therapeutic dialogue becomes frozen.

It is helpful to think of the therapist's *mobile identification* with the patient. This term captures the fluidity and suppleness of the therapist's engagement, while also implying the constancy and comprehensiveness of the therapist's involvement.

5.

Immature Aggression: The Sworn Enemy of the Loving Self

Tom, my seventy-six-year-old, male patient, who'd been coming to me twice a week for several years, asked in a recent session, "Do you like me?" In my lexicon, this question really asks, do I love him? I answered honestly that, lately, I have felt safer with him, more empathic toward him, more able to place myself in his shoes, and have found that he is becoming a more loveable person. When I wanted to know what had provoked his question at this particular moment, he replied that his wife had recently told him that he had become more "mellow" since he'd been working with me.

The above episode revealed progress toward the prime objective of our therapy, namely, the actualization of the loving self. This permitted the reduction of a life-impairing bitterness and grief over the death of his forty-five-year-old son.

Tom's son, Stuart, had suffered with a chronic metabolic illness that, if properly managed, would not have constituted a serious threat to life and function. Nevertheless, Stuart died suddenly while driving, and only later did his loved ones become aware that he had been fatally neglecting his condition by not being under a physician's care, and by self-medicating.

After several months of unabated depression, grievously missing his son, the patient started therapy with me on his wife's insistence. Tom's situation was especially hazardous, because he was having suicidal impulses and was an expert marksman with a large gun collection. He was aware from other sources that I have a son who is approximately the same age as his deceased son. Paradoxically, but not counter-intuitively, this fact was comforting to him; but his raw, guilt-laden sorrow continued to ravage his inner world. His guilt was understandable but not justified. He harshly reproached himself for not having taken more active responsibility for Stuart's health, even though Stuart had misled his father about his health care by telling Tom that his illness was being treated by a medical specialist. Also, Tom had lovingly and frequently asked Stuart about his illness and presumed adequate medical care. I suspected that Tom's guilt might have its source in his divorce, which occurred when his children were young. His conscious de-emphasis of the impact his decision had on their young lives alerted me to the possibility of inhibition of the loving self as an important feature of Tom's relational life.

Tom's deceased son was the child of his first marriage. After a few months of therapy, his wife visited me, and, while she agreed that her husband substituted caution and diffidence for transcendent depth in his relationships, she earnestly assured me that Tom is, at his core, a loving person, and that I would gradually learn that this was so. While I concurred with her formulation, at that time I felt that Tom's defensive narcissism foretold much difficult work in order to liberate his loving self.

Until recently, Tom had seemed oblivious to the possibility that his severe guilt over the death of his son was based on guilt over leaving him when he divorced Stuart's mother. Concurrently, I was aware of an uncomfortable but instructive parallel in my own life. Following a death in the family, I received harsh criticism and rejection by some members of my family. Like Tom, I felt entirely innocent of the charges; but I was also gradually able to realize that, although not guilty of actual misdeeds, I was psychologically culpable at the time of the death. With this in mind, I was able to intensify my identification with Tom's depressive self-reproach. I was also able to help him see that older feelings of guilt were powering his guilt over his son's death. With this realization, Tom's pain diminished.

Tom then reported two important dreams: In the first dream, he was in the rear seat of an automobile. A man was driving with a woman beside him in the passenger seat. Tom also had a woman beside him in the back seat. The driver became angry and shot two people in the car immediately ahead. Tom feared the driver would shoot him and his female companion as eyewitnesses. In order to save his life, he emphatically assured the driver that he would not report the crime.

In the second dream, Tom was kissing a woman. He was, in his words, "so in love with her." The woman, in turn, was deeply in love with him. He told her he had only felt this love "once before." He wondered who the woman was. She bore a slight resemblance to someone he had worked with in the past. Tom was profoundly moved by the love he felt in this dream.

Tom's hobbies are gun collecting and target shooting. When we began our work, he was seriously pondering shooting himself. In our work there had been hints, but not enough documentation, of conditions in his early developmental family that could explain the origins of his current raging tendencies. Certainly, he is the homicidal driver in the first dream, and his appeasing back seat stance reveals his continuing fear of his own rage.

Always armed with a small gun in his pocket, from time to time Tom would tell me that if an assailant ever approached him, he would give that person a warning, but if disobeyed, he would shoot to kill. These announcements had a macho flavor. Later, however, Tom revealed that, whenever away from home, he suffered severe fears of dangerous attack, and carried a weapon to allay anxiety.

Although Tom has never expressed any open aggression toward me, throughout the earlier period of therapy he voiced various complaints about my effectiveness, the futility of therapy, the inconvenience of our schedule, and similar gripes. Now, with the recent emergence and acknowledgement of a more loving regard toward each other, I'm able to appreciate that his previous attitudes pointed to his underlying fury. At the same time, his vulnerable self projected this fury onto me, protecting himself from my murderous potential through the compromise of niggling complaints, similar to his self-protection in the first dream. Basically, his intimidated, repressed, genuine loving self lived in dire fear of his angry, destructive, false self. My ability to uncover and free his loving self posed an immediate threat to his angry self.

My speculative impression is that Tom's deepest fury involves his mother. His hazy references to her suggest an irritable dismissal of her as inadequate to the task of mothering, hence his devaluing attitudes toward me and the therapy. By contrast, parallel to the current loving advancements he has achieved in his marriage and his therapy, I assume he is experiencing a cautious recovery of intense loving feelings toward his mother—the love he felt "only once before," referred to in the second dream.

The presumed difficulties of his early years may have induced great anger toward his mother. It seems quite likely that Tom's profound grief for his son is strongly linked to the deep ambivalence toward his mother.

Tom is the youngest of five children. His closest sibling is ten years his senior. He believes his mother consented to have a fifth child only to please his father. While Tom believes his mother loved him, he also believes she resented him and neglected him emotionally.

I, too, am the youngest of a large family, culturally similar to Tom's, a circumstance that enhances my empathic identification with him. I know whereof he seethes, and participate, through my own endless but muted ambivalence, in the intimate sharing of his grief.

Dreaming in Common

We might even say that Tom's dreams express our common unconscious relational dilemmas. If we assume that the origins of these dreams are now embedded in the therapeutic relationship and its inter-subjective essence, as well as rooted in Tom's early development and his current life, then we may reasonably assume some co-authorship has taken place, through my subordinated subjective participation.

The first dream portrayed the ongoing process of increasing love and declining aggression. Tom was able to readily appreciate that the murderous driver in the front seat and the loving person in the back seat are both aspects of himself, his hostile false self and his intimidated loving self.

When tragedy strikes a family, it permanently alters the family process and the relationship of all of its members. In Tom's case the loving self has emerged from the shadows, and his loving attitude toward all his intimates, including his love for himself, has grown. His defensive narcissism has receded, but not without a struggle. In addition, and perhaps most tellingly, he now permits me to enjoy a safer and more loving experience of him in our therapy. Through inter-subjective exploration of past sources of rage, guilt, inhibition, narcissism, and ambivalence, Tom's loving self is achieving actualization.

More Evidence for the Suppression of the Loving Self

Further developments in this case provide even more compelling evidence that Tom's loving self was being subdued by the hostile self, and his aggression was being used as a defense against love. Highlights of this process are illuminated by the following dreams, which he related about ten days after the two previously described dreams:

1. Stuart is lying on the floor, while Tom rubs his back. Stuart's body feels warm and alive, but Tom knows he is "gone."

2. Tom is in bed and knows he is dying. He says, "I'm going to die in July." (He noted that his father had died on the date of the dream.)

Four days later, Tom had another dream:

3. He wants to take his son into his health club, even though Stuart is not a member. Tom finds a way to surreptitiously bring his son into the club, and they go to the pool. He then falls asleep while Stuart is in the water. Tom awakes with a start, to see if Stuart is okay. He fears that he has not been taking care of his son, and feels guilt over neglecting his child.

Obviously, these dreams announce the continuing wish that Stuart were still living, and Tom's ongoing self-reproach over his son's death. They also hint at his special guilt over leaving his marriage when his child was young and dependent. Furthermore, the dreams point to deep and as yet unrevealed aspects of his relationship to his father.

In the sessions following these revelatory incidents, remarkable new developments occurred. Tom and I began exploring, with greater frequency and depth, how he was using anger as a chronic defense against his loving self. I had correctly interpreted the dream about the gun-toting driver as an important harbinger of imminent changes. In that dream, Tom clearly portrayed his hostile self, as well as his authentic, loving self's fearful and appeasing behavior toward his own rage. It was also becoming increasingly evident how, over the years, while his loving self has continued seeking abiding, fulfilling love, his anger and fear have led him, instead, away from such fulfillment and into perpetual discontent.

More evidence: Tom has a dream in which he is aware that he is dying and knows when he will die. The dream is obviously connected to his son's death, but his main association of the dream to the death of his father thirty-nine years earlier indicates a more philosophical, less bitter acceptance of the life-death cycle.

Tom reminded me that when we began therapy, he was seriously considering suicide, and that, via his huge gun collection, he had ample lethal resources on hand. I explained that, in the past, I had often felt his rage and was not able to experience the sense of safety that would have allowed me to relax and feel closer and more vulnerable with him.

He seemed shocked at this, and quickly reassured me that I had never been in any danger in his presence. I also hastened to remind him that, lately, I have felt much closer and safer with him emotionally.

Changing Tom's Story

I asked him whether his hostile, false self had its source in his chronic feelings that his mother was not deeply invested in him. He repeated that he was the youngest of five children, and I reminded him that I, too, was the youngest of five. We acknowledged that he was separated in age by ten years from his nearest sibling, which could have left him feeling isolated or distant from the family.

Furthermore, he had been told that his mother wanted no more children, but consented to conceive one in order to please his father, who yearned for another little kid around the house. I pointed out to him that his natural yearning for abundant love was thwarted, generating fury and guilt. This yearning also established a narrative theme in which love was sought after but never sustained, just as his experience of love from his mother couldn't be sustained. In recent weeks, however, his "mellower" attitude and my greater closeness to him pointed to the important revision of his story: that he was unloved by his mother, permitting a reduction of angry feelings and self-thwarting behavior, and, perhaps, leading to a contented, faithful relationship.

Tom then assured me that although he always carries a loaded gun, I have never been in any danger from him, something I was not consciously aware of, although he'd mentioned it early on in therapy. I asked him, "Are you carrying a gun today?" He nodded and produced a small, loaded pistol from his pocket, then handed it to me. I held it gingerly for a moment and gave it back to him. He then announced that he would no longer bring weapons to our sessions, which led me to comment that his loving self was, by all appearances, gaining ascendancy over his fearful, aggressive false self.

The Triumph of the Loving Self

During two more years of arduous work in therapy, Tom's defensive distance from me gradually subsided, accompanied by the emergence of recurring demands from him that I be more warm and loving, since he felt unsure about the steadiness and reliability of my warmth. At the same time, a haughty flavor in his attitude to me decreased, leaving him in a vulnerable, needy state. My response was characterized by a greater sense of identity with him, including an unprecedented recovery of memories of my very early childish tantrums with my mother. This experience correlated to an interesting dream Tom told me one day:

> "I am with my father. I tell him that he can play an 80 year-old man, but not a younger person. And I tell him further that I can take the role of a younger person, like a 65-year-old."

As we discussed this dream, we agreed that it revealed a resolution of suffering in the father-son relationship to the father, to me, and to his son. A strengthening enhancement of the loving identification in all three of these relationships seemed to have occurred. Additionally, the implied reduction of anxiety in these relationships promised more integration of the major dissociated elements of anger in his unconscious relation to his mother.

While the events of each therapy are varied and unique, there is a relentless constancy to all therapy: that is the struggle of the vulnerable, intimidated loving self to achieve actualization, with the important corollary of relational fulfillment. This case, I believe, indicates that such progress can occur at all stages of a person's life.

I selected this case for this chapter because it offers an exceptional portrayal of immature hostility, intimidating and stifling the fearful loving self. Here, I am referring to the remarkable dream of the murderous man (the false hostile self) in the driver's seat and the cringing man (the loving self) in the back seat of the automobile.

Our shared experience has been a lively period of liberation of the loving self, arising from Tom's *struggle for recognition* from a mother (therapist), who seemed otherwise occupied. And I feel gratitude to Tom for a major advance in my own relational maturation.

6.

The Therapist's Subordinated Subjectivity and the Loving Self

Without the therapist's suitably subordinated subjectivity psychotherapy fails. Psychotherapy always requires the activity of the therapist's subjectivity. But this subjectivity must be attuned and responsive to the patient's needs, and is thus neither obtrusive nor intrusive. Even for therapists who accord importance to their own subjectivity only when it becomes more or less obvious, the sustained necessity of their underlying subjective experience remains.

If the therapist's subjectivity becomes blatant and clamorous, it actually impedes therapeutic progress—this is unmastered subjectivity out of control. Obviously, this is not subordinated subjectivity. It is therefore not capable of functioning as searching subjectivity. Under such conditions of unmastered subjectivity, the therapist's narcissistic vulnerability is excessive, and the welcoming receptiveness of the therapist's subjectivity is diminished or abolished. The patient's subjectivity is then either rejected or exploited.

On the other hand, when the therapist accepts, even welcomes, his own subjectivity, warts and all, this subjectivity becomes modulated, plastic, and responsive to the therapist's therapeutic intentions. His subjectivity, in the

Therapeutic situation, is subordinated to the therapeutic exigencies. The therapist's narcissistic neediness drops to a suitably low level, and his subjectivity, we may say, is at the service of the patient. The therapist's primary narrative themes remain active, but can now receive and embrace the patient's equivalent theme, rather than twisting or repudiating it.

A Universe of Themes

Searching subjectivity requires the therapist to make room for the patient. The attenuated, but nonetheless authentic, subjectivity of the therapist becomes a searching subjectivity, but not in a conscious or calculated way. The subjective needs of the therapist have lost their urgency and, in a genuine manner, can serve the needs of the other. This does not require the wholesale abandonment of the therapist's own needs. The therapist can thereby identify with the patient and can carry the patient's painful theme into a transformative interaction with the therapist's theme. The commingling of the respective themes of patient and therapist effects major change in the patient's theme and a lesser, but still beneficial change, in the therapist.

The above reference to the engagement of two themes, one from the therapist and one from the patient, does not exclude multiple thematic interactions occurring simultaneously. All these connect with one another and are reciprocally influential. My view is that in each of us, several developmentally derived relational themes are active—and exist in an endlessly vast pool of potential narrative themes that are as extensive as the human universe itself. So each of us necessarily and unconsciously exerts decisive editorial influence and establishes a handful of salient narrative themes that constitute the accessible self. It is within this arbitrarily selective self-defined and self-defining sphere that the manifest and submerged therapeutic dialogue goes on.

Each self, based on its constituent relational themes, builds itself and changes through the process first described. But this change is only possible through human relationships. Thus, in therapy, we reduce the field to a manageable complexity, consisting of a few leading narrative themes in the patient and in the therapist. Essentially, these include parents and siblings, as well as an occasionally relevant other. As the patient's blatantly needy self engages the therapist's more quietly needy self, the therapeutic process moves forward. Each self is the aggregate of the person's main relational themes. The self is always unstable enough to change as these inter-subjective events occur.

Fortunately, an optimal therapeutic relationship takes time, which enables multiple salient themes to be in the foreground or in the background as the therapeutic relationship shifts and unfolds.

A New Process, A New Relationship

Conventionally, we have believed that as the therapy moved on, different transferences (mother, father, sibling) would be projected on to the therapist. The patient would mistakenly assume the therapist was behaving like one of these figures from the past, while the therapist, with imperfect yet laudable stability, maintained a gentle objectivity.

We have now realized that our conventional impression was incorrect, and the patient's insistence that the therapist was not maintaining a basic objectivity was more correct than our belief that the patient was only projecting some essentially internal process on to the therapist. Instead, we assume that the therapist is always engaged inter-subjectively with the patient. Furthermore, the patient is correct when he or she insists that the therapist has this or that emotion-laden attitude toward him or her. Of course the patient's precise impression of the therapist's emotional engagement, its exact quality and intensity, may be distorted, but the patient's basic assumption is correct. This is the therapist's subordinated and searching subjectivity at work. It is often true that when the therapist achieves some clarity as to the basic meaning of his emotional involvement with the patient, he becomes capable of formulating and sharing with the patient the most fluent and influential interpretations of the patient's inner experience.

This intimate interaction of the subjectivities of patient and therapist entails a continuous mutual identification. Shared identification means that each party is always having a subjective experience that includes the subjective experience of the other—sometimes this may be consciously felt but not consciously understood. At other times identification with the other is not amply appreciated. The therapist's identification is therefore continuous and indispensable for the therapeutic process. Identification should be the defining term for the therapist's basic therapeutic experience. This is the therapeutic event in which the therapist is the patient and remains himself. It is symbiosis with separateness. For the wary patient to whom intimacy may threaten engulfment or devastating loss, this therapeutic identification provides the basis for hope and growth. It is neither too much nor too little.

Jennifer is a fifty-five-year-old businesswoman who told me, in her first telephone call, that she was looking for therapy with an "old Jew." In my wry amusement I told her that she had come to the right place, and we began a twice weekly therapy schedule.

Jennifer had told me that she was seeking therapy due to severe anxiety arising from a complicated business deal that had resulted in a lawsuit with a judgment of many millions of dollars against her. She had now appealed the adverse judgment and was nervously hoping for a reversal. But the uncertainty was corroding her well-being. She had been in psychotherapy previously with a female therapist, and believed they had worked mainly on her problems with her mother, while knowingly disregarding her equally troublesome relationship with her father.

Jennifer had a dramatic streak. In fateful tones she reported that she was conceived the night before her oldest brother was accidentally killed on the street in their provincial Argentine town. Her older sister, who had been in charge of the killed brother, became a kind of family pariah, and was "exiled" to Italy when she was an adolescent. Jennifer developed mixed feelings of being an angel of death as well as a replacement for the original. She also felt that the strange circumstance of her conception may have explained her father's relational reticence toward her.

Jennifer was disappointed by her father's alcoholic withdrawal from effective parenting and by the adaptive problems of her three brothers. (Her sisters seemed to be less important or less threatening to her.) Although her opening remark about an old Jew had suggested that she was looking for a solution to the estrangement from her dead father, our meetings were initially dominated by the omnipresent mother. It was as though unfinished maternal business had to be completed before the father could become the center of the therapeutic process.

In this early period, I experienced an unusual kind of emotion. It was a bearable but intense feeling of poignancy that would fluctuate in intensity. It was related to sadness, yet it also connoted loving intimacy. When I mentioned it to Jennifer, she acknowledged her shared experience, and we agreed that it was important, but no definitive explanation was articulated. I felt that she and I joined in a benign union that could reproduce in each of us various familial relational conditions that clamored to be re-experienced and resolved. She told me that I have excellent receptors, which is true, but the whole truth was not contained in that partial explanation. Perhaps in the gentle reality of our emerging dialogue, we liberated the excluded parental love (maternal and paternal) that had been obstructed by the mother's heedless feminine aggression and the father's defeated masculine withdrawal. We knew our dialogical intimacy had soft power, although it was not clearly understood.

The singular emotion convinced me, and I believe Jennifer also, that we had awakened a sleeping emotional giant and that unprecedented psychological changes were happening. We could not yet do more than understand that powerful mutative forces were being created that arose from our difference: her need and my expertise, but which had more elemental meaning that could not be subsumed to our difference. In other words, my expertise included my needs—although these needs of mine were subordinated to hers, and thereby became the searching subjectivity so necessary to therapy.

By subordination, I mean that during the therapeutic sessions the therapist's subjective experience is primarily at the service of the patient. The therapist's thoughts may be sketchy or detailed, the feelings attending memories and fantasies may be mild or intense. But the therapist regularly perceives that his subjective processes have important linkage to the psychological processes occurring simultaneously in the patient. From this the therapist usually gains richer insight into the patient's current relational conflicts and defenses.

We should always appreciate the importance of the therapist's visceral experience of the ongoing psychological process. But in this case, a new level of refinement and power of this phenomenon occurred.

Jennifer and I always knew when the described emotion increased or diminished. From time to time we would mention it; usually, however, that was unnecessary. We shared a continuous, fluctuant emotional experience. But she talked of the past events of her life and current events, while I also was silently involved with my own subordinated life themes (in all their emotion-ladenness) and made interpretive observations that invariably felt fitting, helpful, and relieving to her.

Certain recurring patterns were becoming clearer and less dangerous. She knew she lived in a world polarized between the powerful mother and the defeated father. However, she also began to realize that behind the presenting mother another frantic, confused, disorganized mother existed. Similarly, hidden within the overtly depressed, ineffectual father was a loving, focused man.

Jennifer achieved a breathtaking awareness that these four parental orientations were the cornerstones of her most basic narrative themes, i.e., those stories that defined her inner life with her parents and are central to her self. Multiple beneficial changes were occurring: less dismay over and more love for her mother, less defensive impatience with her husband and brothers, heightened yearning for the early thrill of being with her effective father. As part of this eruption of fulfillment, she shared with me her belief that, even as an old man, I am at the summit of my productive enthusiasm for life. I experienced this as a new truth that crystallized while being stated—a loving validation inevitably consequent to the unique productivity of our work.

The gloomy counterpoint to all these exhilarating changes was the apparent continuing impasse with Jennifer's older daughter, twenty-six years of age. The young woman was obviously stuck in a severe developmental crisis of a chronic nature. Jennifer experienced painful inhibition with her daughter and was helplessly aware that it was a virtually exact replica of the severe inhibition in her relationship with her father. Jennifer's inability to relate constructively to her daughter could not change until her own inner impasse with her father melted and dissolved.

The complex but dialogically unelaborated father-daughter problem was actually becoming more accessible. And richly pertinent dreams occurred:

1. Jennifer is in a session with me—but I'm Paul Mazursky. She is lying down, and her school record is on the wall. She is looking for the equivalent of an A+, so she assumes it's the wrong record—but she doesn't feel anxious about it. Then we move to the kitchen. She says, "We cannot stop here." I say it is OK. The homosexual lover of my son walks by to learn if he's approved. Also, there are a couple of male twins, wearing circus-like shirts—they are my twins.

2. Jennifer is in Shanghai with her former business partner, who is powerful in Shanghai. She feels empowered. A car contains miniature samples of things to sell. She is preparing items for display and sale.

In her first meeting with me, Jennifer indicated a knowledge of my son in his career and marriage, which thereby emphasizes the symbolism entailed in dreaming of my son as a homosexual. In the dream she is rediscovering the deep inevitably erotic love of father and son and in her case, the profound but repressed love of daughter and father. The process is intense but incomplete. Yet, as in the second dream, she is feeling "empowered." The twins are Jennifer and her mother, Jennifer and her daughter, she and I, my son and I, Jennifer and my son.

In the therapy, Jennifer and I are reconfiguring her relationship to her father, herself, and to her daughter. Of essential importance, I inevitably rework my relationship to my father and to myself, but of course this process is suitably subordinated to our shared experience, and it is not discussed with the patient.

Here is another example of how the therapist's subordinated subjectivity functions as searching subjectivity in the therapeutic experience. A fifty-year-old patient began his sessions by reporting something he recalled after our last meeting. He was a child; he entered a room and saw his father with his hand down the dress of his father's sister, Angela. As he told me this, the patient shook his head in dismay over the sexual irresponsibility endemic in his childhood family. This new memory was especially interesting for several reasons, which I will discuss.

The patient entered therapy with me because a minor traffic accident had activated intense anxiety, hypochondriasis, and depression— accompanied by the eruption of previously repressed painful memories of serial molestations by his father and possibly other men. Over several months, incident after incident was remembered—to his horror and disgust. In his previous psychotherapy, before he remembered any of the sexual trauma, his first therapist had emphatically assured him that his parents had been perfectly adequate parents—despite his long-standing history of anger to and avoidance of his father and his disappointed feelings toward his mother. Later, he saw another analyst, with whom he discovered various memories of paternal sexual abuse. Even then he continued having troubled feelings regarding his family—hatred for his father and uncertainty toward his mother, feeling strongly but vaguely that unfinished business remained. He believes this therapist prematurely terminated his therapy for reasons that are unclear. He wonders if the therapist was developing Alzheimer's.

As our dialogue unfolded over several months, he plaintively and repeatedly wondered why this ostensibly good father could have done such terrible things. The memory of his father illicitly touching his aunt had heuristic value for both of us. We had already discussed the frequency with which child molesters have been themselves molested as children. Therefore, this instance of brother-sister incest pointed us to the likelihood of severe sexual disturbance in the father's family—including probable molestation of him as a child.

Of particular interest here is my dream that occurred one or two nights prior to this last session. I recall only a fragment: I see a man and a woman in bed—it is as though she entered his bed unbidden. She was naked, light-haired, and somewhat overweight. She encouraged his advances to her, although they both seemed indifferent, then she was gone. Initially, the dream baffled me, but I decided to remember it. During the patient's report of his father's hand on his sister's breast, I was eerily reminded of furtive erotic contacts during childhood with my sisters—minor touchings, and probably abetted by my sisters. I then realized that my dream revealed childhood incestuous desire for my sisters and that these desires were interacting with the patient's.

These memories informed me of the powerful inter-subjective process going on. An important narrative theme of mine is my ambivalent and unconsciously eroticized relationship to my sisters.

It became clear that this underlying issue of mine, suitably subordinated, was playing an indispensable searching role in our therapeutic relationship. My dream, revealing erotic involvement with a sister, resonated unconsciously with the patient, and it probably facilitated the emergence of the instructive memory of his father's incestuous act with a sister. In my experience with the patient, I was identifying with the abused little boy, and I was also the father, playing with the sister-son. In the fusion of the therapeutic process, my clarification of an active underlying theme of mine also enabled the patient to achieve a very helpful clarification of his own. I did not discuss my dream or my association with the patient.

This opening into the father's neurotic experience seemed to lift the patient's spirits. His mien had previously been one of discouragement and despair. Now, he showed more smiling hopefulness. We agreed that the change resulted from the new awareness of the transgenerational significance of the father's sexual neurosis. Perhaps it even enabled the patient to achieve some mature understanding that he too was driven by childhood devils of forbidden sexuality. Even in such a grim tale, room exists for the loving self.

Through the Looking Glass

This profoundly inter-subjective event instructs us in different ways. For example, it convinces me that the patient and I are reenacting the hideous drama that shattered his childhood and damaged, but did not destroy, his adult years. In the deeper strata of our shared experience, each of us is both violator and victim. This can occur with therapeutic benefit because he also experiences me as maternally warm, protecting, and helpful. The safe maternal embrace enables us to relive the darkness of the past, illuminate it, while realizing it is truly past—not present.

The possibility of forgiveness of his father is definitely not on the therapeutic table. While we continue to define his father as a very sick man who sinned in the most venal way, a beneficial softening of his earlier rigid stance has also occurred. He knows that his father endowed him with high intelligence and that his father effectively stimulated the patient's involvement in high culture. He feels a muted gratitude to him for these bestowals. By chance, I have some familiarity with the father's native socio-cultural background, and through such discussions, we have partially contextualized the father as a social being—tempering the demonization—without forgiveness.

To a gratifying extent, the patient's past bitter, victimized feelings no longer soil the satisfactions of his relational life. Father as smirking evil genius now is replaced by a weak, destructive person whose intellectual pretensions barely mask his seamy truth.

7.

Dreams, Narrative Theme, and the Loving Self

The surpassing importance for psychotherapy of the interactive relationship of dreams, narrative theme, and loving self is the subject of this chapter. These processes are invariably active in every psychotherapy, even when they go unnoticed by patient and therapist. Dreams may be unremembered, narrative theme undefined, and loving self unarticulated; nevertheless, their indispensable interactions occur. The following pages will explain these covert processes.

Dreams reveal the salient narrative theme; this theme reflects the painful life story that keeps the loving self unfulfilled. Understanding this story permits a transformation of the theme, resulting in the liberation of the loving self.

Dreams

Since dreams occupy approximately five percent of our total lifetime, it behooves us under any circumstances to know more about our dreams. Typically, an adult dreams for sixty to eighty minutes each night. Dreams occur for fifteen to twenty minutes at the end of each sleep cycle lasting seventy-five to ninety minutes. Dreams are recalled at the instant of awakening, and most are forgotten almost as quickly. But the special circumstance of therapy makes attention to dreams a matter of special importance. A dream usually tells a story, or at least we dreamers tend to attach our important life stories to our dreams. When the patient thinks and talks about her dreams in therapy, she becomes increasingly aware of her own life stories—also called narrative themes or relational themes.

The following clinical examples will illustrate the above points and show how dreams express the dreamer's narrative theme.

Clinging to the Story

Riva, a fifty-five-year-old woman, was driven to therapy by a marital crisis: her husband had recently discovered that Riva was sexually involved with another man. Her husband became furious, drank heavily, and was physically assaultive. Riva became anxious and depressed. She is from a working class family. She holds an advanced degree and is in a successful business. She is the only family member with more than a high school education. During her initial session, Riva reported an astonishing piece of history: at age six, she returned one day from school and discovered her mother in the kitchen attempting to amputate the arm of her three-year-old brother with a butcher knife. It was a terrifying scene, the mother was hospitalized, and the victim had a three-inch laceration from which he still bears a scar. When the mother recovered from her violent state, she returned to the family, and life went on, seemingly as before. While Riva was unaware of any post traumatic effects, she did develop a generalized feeling of distaste for her family.

A few sessions later Riva reported a first dream, then a few days later, a second dream:

1. Riva is with her younger brother in a doctor's office. The brother is having his abdomen cut open for a liver biopsy. The dreamer wonders why the abdomen is being cut open for a procedure that requires only a needle biopsy of the liver. The doctor tells the horrified dreamer that she will be next.

2. Riva has to undergo chemotherapy for a liver problem. Other patients are there. She is told that she will have a series of these treatments for six to twelve months. She is concerned about side effects, but she is comforted by the fact that she is obtaining needed treatment.

These dreams possess remarkable expository power. They reveal the continuing dread of the homicidal mother, the persistence of this dread regarding the violent husband and the transfer of this fear to the psychotherapist—who will violate her body by exposing her thoughts. On the hopeful side, there the second dream, in which she is receiving necessary treatment by the doctor (therapist).

The revelatory quality of these two typically naïve early dreams of therapy as trauma is very impressive. The narrative theme, barely disguised, is that it is her fate to live with a dangerous mother, whether she be the mother of childhood, or a later mother surrogate (husband or therapist). From the therapeutic standpoint, these dreams have almost pellucid informative quality.

A few weeks after reporting these dreams, Riva abruptly ended therapy, offering no explanation. I believe that her fear of intimacy was so enormous that it precluded a therapeutic dialogue, which would force her to encounter the terrifying relationship to her mother. (This therapeutic problem of realizing and integrating the hated and feared parent in oneself is addressed in detail in another chapter.)

The Power of Dreams

Dreams can communicate the central story that dominates and damages a person's life. Potentially, central life themes can change, but only if they become open rather than covert, conscious rather than unconscious, actively engaged rather than passively submitted to. Life story, developmental theme, or, preferably, narrative theme, is the nucleus of a person's psychological relational life. Each person has as many narrative themes as she has basic developmental relationships. These coalesce to establish the self, an organized aggregate of these family derived narrative themes. Since the self is composed of these salient relational themes, relational events in an individual's current life will inevitably resonate with the narrative theme pertinent to the present situation. The loving effectiveness of the relevant theme will determine whether the person engages the event successfully.

The relational core of human experience and the key relational themes determine relational success or failure, growth or retardation. However, this account is somewhat simplistic and does not acknowledge the incalculable complexity of an individual's relational world. The oversimplification is unavoidable, because each person lives an endless, limitless number of narrative themes. Our attention must be limited to the small number of salient themes that are dominant in each person's life. To paraphrase Pierre Bourdieu, although each person inhabits the world, the world inhabits each person. This is indispensable background awareness.

The foreground, that is, our impinging consciousness, consists of a small number of salient themes. These appropriately emerge as the focus of therapeutic attention. Reliving these themes in the therapeutic dialogue stimulates their transformation, with the inevitable enhancement of their loving potentials.

The following case shows how a salient narrative theme reveals itself through dreams, and how its virulence can be greatly reduced as a result of successful therapy.

The Story We Tell Ourselves

Thomas is a 39 year-old physician who spent several years in intensive psychotherapy with me. He sought therapy because of a serious relational problem and an increasing depression. He was born in Mexico City to professional parents—their first child. He reported that he was a happy little boy, but he had recurring hazily painful memories of severe conflict between his incompatible parents.

When Thomas was six years old, his little world fell apart. He now had a younger brother, age three. But by this time, the parents could no longer bear living together. Abruptly, they separated, and they divided the children. Thomas was taken by his father, while his younger brother remained with the mother. And, further complicating Thomas' young life, his father moved with the patient to Los Angeles, where he established himself, remarried, and did attempt to meet the boy's emotional needs.

Superficially, Thomas made a successful adaptation to the disruption of his Mexican life, to the loss of his mother and his little brother. He became an excellent student. Socially, however, he was painfully reserved, and he greeted friendly overtures from peers with exceptional caution—as though it would be unsafe to immerse himself and become a vigorous participant in relationships. Occasional reunions with his mother and younger brother suffered the same gloomy pall, and when he returned home to father, he would remain in this painful condition for several weeks.

The following three dreams typify Thomas' dream work that contributed greatly to our mobilization and reduction of his life problems.

1. Thomas is a junior physician in a small, successful group medical practice. The two senior physicians become bitter enemies, and the group dissolves. One of the seniors, a female gynecolo-

gist, asks the patient's close friends to join her in another practice. Thomas feels deeply wounded, inadequate, and very angry.

2. The patient tries out for his school's baseball team, but he doesn't make the starting lineup. However, his close friend becomes a starter. Patient feels unlovable, inadequate, sad.

3. Thomas falls in love. Initially, the young woman is very interested. She is sexually responsive and eager to be with him. However, without warning, she ends the relationship, telling him she is now in love with someone else. Thomas is crushed, very sad.

These three transparent dreams constitute a sampling of dozens of similar dreams that occurred in the course of our work together. Although superficially varied, the dreams express a consistent underlying theme: the collapse of his childhood family, the loss of his mother and brother, and the consequent inner agony. These dreams point to Thomas' narrative theme: his relationships are fated to fail, he will lose his beloved, and a sibling-like person will succeed where Thomas fails. Our dialogue was replete with such real and fantasized events—including the patient's dismal expectations of the outcome of our relationship. Instead, however, through our therapeutic efforts, the dominance of this grim relational theme subsided, and he became fulfilled in love and in the other sectors of his life. Together, we strengthened and freed his loving self.

Stories Buried in Dreams

Despite important differences in the two preceding patients, a noteworthy common quality is present in their dreams: the basic narrative theme of each person can be readily recognized when their respective histories become known. Also, both dreamers produced dreams with intense emotional content, although the source of the painful emotion was initially unconscious. The premature termination in one case precludes progress, whereas in the other case, a rich and profitable discovery of unconscious meaning was the basis of the patient's recovery of his loving self. This led to abundant intimate and occupational happiness. In the following case, the core theme of the dream is less obvious, but when made clear, reveals its powerful relevance to the dreamer's life world.

Here is the dream: "My therapist exerts pressure on me, and I fall into a hypnotic state. In my lowered state, I am actually pushed, by the therapist, to a lower level, a basement—large black rocks fill the space. The atmosphere is unpleasant—even ominous." End of dream.

David felt anger. "I am depressed. Now my anxiety is gone, and I feel awful. It's connected to that dream." David's remark had a reproachful tone, as though my longstanding attention to his anxiety and my recent efforts to cultivate transference awareness had now borne poisoned fruit. Looking frightened and resentful, he seemed to blame me for my focus on his anxiety and my attention to transference. Previous therapists had not made an issue of his anxiety, nor had they ever discussed the therapeutic relationship in terms of his basic developmental family relationships. I upset the apple cart by deviating from familiar therapist behavior.

The hypnotizing therapist represents me—pushing him into regression. I have forced him to realize that in his unconscious he has carried the heavy burden of the rocks—immovable and immutable. These rocks represent his chronic mother problem. He could never be certain that he had pleased his mother. So he was always self-effacing, tense, anxious about pleasing others, hesitant to assert his will. He is now much more aware of his chronic anxiety, but he is also aware that his anxiety protects him from depression.

David's rueful glance conveyed a definite message: Unlike his previous therapists, I tampered with his fragile equilibrium by loosening his anxiety, releasing his depression. Obviously, this was not the first time David had been depressed. However, what was new was his conscious linkage of his anxiety and his depression, as well as his important self-interpretation that anxiety protected him from the depression. His attitude was that we should have left well enough alone; he would have been happier with the status quo ante.

David blamed me for being like his mother when I pointed out his anxiety and expected him to change—like mother, I was not satisfied with the original. At the outset, he did not realize this was negative mother transference to me: In fact, prior to this experience, he had never recognized, nor had I interpreted any transference to me. In all his previous years of therapy with other therapists, apparently, no transferential issues had ever been discussed.

Uncovering the Loving Self

The path from the jagged upland of anxiety to the fertile plains of the loving self often takes us through the dark detours of depression. But it is a trail well-taken, as this dreamer's clinical story reveals. David is a middle-aged man, whose life was fraught with anxiety and menaced by the deeper threat of depression. His journey finally took him to his loving self.

David had been in psychotherapy from late adolescence in his foreign home city, then later with other therapists, most recently with me, for the past several years. A sophisticated, successful professional, he was recovering from the fairly recent death of his mother, and was now struggling with the increasing dementia of his aging father, who had come to be with him from their distant homeland. He also suffered unpredictable and unfair attacks from his unstable, bipolar younger sister, and was painfully preoccupied with the occupational and relational struggles of his grown offspring. Beyond this, David acknowledged some phobic fear that arose under special circumstances, particularly flying. On the other hand, his marriage, though turbulent in its early phase, had matured into a stable source of security and support in his life.

David's therapy with me occurred in three phases: First, we worked on his guilt-soaked resentment of his father and sister for their blaming and devaluing attitudes toward him. He could also see that his worries and disappointments with his children arose in part from conflicts with his sister and father. In time, our focus, within the safety of our dialogue, led to the abatement of tension over father and sister, accompanied by similar improvements in David's relationship with his children.

The next phase was characterized by intense feelings of rejection by his mother. In this period of the therapy, David endlessly reviewed and re-experienced the intimate, ambivalent relationship to his mother, in which he continually tried to please her, but never succeeded. Not surprisingly, he also relived these issues with his wife, children, and friends.

The third phase was characterized by the upsurge of negative mother transference to me, through which he came to realize that his chronic anxiety concealed his deep depression over maternal rejection. This was the culmination of successful therapy. David was again able to concentrate and enjoy activities, like travel, that had been impaired by his anxiety.

Anxiety and Depression

Anxiety and depression share a long, complex, and significant history. To this day, their connection possesses clinical and commercial importance. Therapists often encounter co-extant anxiety and depression; or anxiety and depression that alternate as primary manifest affect; or anxiety that covers an inferred underlying depression. This last situation is the focus of this case: abundant anxiety that conceals an abiding deep and barely discernible depression.

Not surprisingly, the pharmaceutical industry has smelled huge profit in the linkage of these two ubiquitous emotional states. The sales pitch runs as follows: *We have been selling you medicine for your disease, "depression." Now, we have a new drug that will also be good for another disease, "anxiety." This new medication cures or ameliorates your second disease, which you may have been unaware of. This marvelous new drug cures or relieves both diseases—you must buy it to take proper care of yourself. Remember: These are diseases, and they require chemical intervention.*

The conscientious therapist holds a skeptical or dismissive attitude toward these profit-driven claims. Such therapists acknowledge the value of medication for some emotional problems, but oppose exaggerated claims. This thoughtful and restrained therapeutic attitude really enjoys a Freudian lineage.

Freud originally regarded anxiety as the unmanaged breakthrough of instinctual force. This was a less subtle and less valid notion of anxiety states than his revised theory of anxiety. He coined the term, *signal anxiety*, meaning that anxiety symptoms indicated that repression of unacceptable affects was failing. In the case presentation discussed above, David first became aware of his sustained anxiety. He then realized that his anxiety warded off his depression. Next, he became depressed. Finally, he resolved his depression and his anxiety. This became possible through the neat piece of transference analysis.

These sequential steps inexorably led to progressive liberation of the loving self. The patient's previous attitudes toward self were those of self-effacement and self-doubt. Similarly, he was apprehensive about the fates of his loved ones, laced with subtle dissatisfaction with their adaptive efforts—as well as his own attempts to lead a fulfilling life. Now he was able to enjoy the richness of his inner being as well as his most valuable intimate relationships.

As mentioned above, David became angry with me for tampering with his anxiety, stating that he had always sensed that beneath his jittery surface lurked depression, which arose from his mother's high expectations, conjoined with her recurring dissatisfaction with David. Even at his birth, he was told, his mother turned away from him into depression because she was so dismayed by his appearance.

It seemed to me that his previous years with various therapists had helped him through the therapists' consistent affirming approach that provided him with a needed corrective emotional experience. But the therapies had never been interpretive of the invasion into his present relationships—including the therapeutic relationship—by unresolved problems originating in his developmental relationships.

Through the dream, he realized that I, the dream therapist, was pushing deeply below his surface of anxiety into the dark, immutable underworld of his depression (the rocks). My dissatisfaction with his anxiety meant that, ironically, I was like the ever-dissatisfied mother. As he realized the mother transference, a bounty of unprecedented benefit occurred. His self-esteem and self-confidence soared.

David's reproachfulness toward me quickly subsided and was replaced by a glowing gratitude. Through realizing that unconsciously he had been reliving the depressing drama with his mother, he could confidently believe in the resolution of his anxiety. He could also recognize that he had not been appreciating the adult autonomy of his offspring, and he could now relinquish the complex reliving with them of his own mother-son conflicts.

Some weeks after these dramatic clinical events, David realized an important additional meaning of the dark rocks in the dream; namely, that he had been *petrified*. Clearly, the rocks represented his twin stumbling blocks: depression and fear.

In this case, an almost welcome situation of chronic anxiety contained underlying depression; in turn, the depression subdued the loving self. The fulfillment of loving potential had to await understanding and removal of the double layering of neurotic symptoms. David's journey brought his loving self out of the rocky basement and into the light.

8.

From Lying Self to Loving Self

Changing a false self (in this case a lying self) into a loving self takes a great deal of time and work. A person who lies in intimacy is unconsciously protecting a fragile and endangered loving self from unbearable pain or destruction. The following case, which demonstrates the arduous process and intimate intricacies of prolonged treatment, lasted well over a decade.

James and Jill

Approximately ten years ago, a tall, willowy, brunette beauty entered my office. She was born in a large Australian city, the descendant of English felons who were forced to emigrate from England in the eighteenth century, and who gained considerable social status in subsequent decades. Jill's father was a professor of hydraulic engineering. Her mother was a housewife. And Jill had a younger sister. The father had a domineering personality, and he ruled the family with an iron fist. Jill reported that this willful behavior drove her mother into a frozen submission—a kind of psychological absenteeism. Even though Jill's father made her his favorite—over mother and sister, Jill longed for her mother to protect her from her father's tyranny. She felt that in withdrawal her mother had fled in order to save her own skin, and had thus betrayed Jill. Father designated the younger sister as bad, and she dutifully went on to become an unstable failure in both her love life and her career. Father essentially made Jill the woman of the family; and she then became the feminine oedipal victor, but what a Pyrrhic victory! Although the father anointed her, the cost was prohibitive: she had to obey her father unquestioningly, disdain her mother, and offer complete fealty. Father bestowed and withdrew love capriciously. And frequently he would go on alcoholic rampages that confused and terrified Jill. Furthermore, he demanded that he be referred to only as Father. References such as Dad, Daddy, Pop, Poppa, he and him were strictly forbidden.

As a child, Jill was tiny, skinny and timid. (And ever since then she has falsely perceived herself as small and frail—despite her tall, handsome presence.) Heedless of Jill's developmental needs, Father forced her to attend summer camp at an early age. There she languished, as Father ignored her plaintive pleas to come home. At school, she did poorly, and was placed in a class with the less successful students, where she felt proud and happy to be the smartest of the dumb. Eventually, a perceptive teacher realized that she was very bright but very fearful, and she was reassigned to a more suitable class.

As Jill grew through latency, puberty, and adolescence, she developed impressive compensatory skills as a tutor and laboratory assistant. With these resources she earned considerable sums of money. For the most part, however, she was lonely, living by her wits, racked with shame and envy as she watched from the sidelines of social life, imagining herself still small and weak—even though she was growing into a tall, beautiful adolescent.

During this prolonged relational misery, Jill excelled scholastically and moved steadily up the academic ladder, capping her success by graduating first in her class at a major engineering school. Her career achievements quickly multiplied, and she became famous in a large region of Australia by conceiving and implementing innovative agricultural and housing programs that protected the rights of the aborigines, the "little people." In this way she expressed her defeated mother's habitus, a buried penchant for social justice. Later, she moved to the U.S.A. Since then, she has been an academic, working in the field of social engineering.

When Jill was twelve, she fell in love. He was a good-looking and popular boy. She was smitten. Eventually, he claimed her by kissing her. She promptly fled. This was the prototypical event of a chronically recurring pattern: she would seek unconditional love from a male who symbolized the loving father she never had, and then she would flee because of terror of commitment. In adolescence, despite her father's opposition, she began therapy—for which she assumed financial responsibility. She had been in therapy almost continuously since that time. Despite Jill's abundant developmental memories, until recently it was always very difficult for her to connect her current intimate life with developmental issues in an experientially meaningful manner.

At age twenty-five, Jill married. Her husband was an accomplished and attractive young man—also from Australia. The marriage lasted and the couple had a daughter. The marital relationship, however, only limped along. Ever discontented, Jill was driven recurringly to find romantic stimulation in other relationships with men. She sought to be loved by a very desirable man, but when she won him, she was no longer interested and would only long for the durable and reliable affection of her husband. Of course, these extramarital adventures required endless deceits, and resourceful Jill was magisterial in orchestrating the complex requirements of her double, or sometimes even triple life. Since profit rather than probity is the bottom line in the business world, Jill's lies and sleights of hand at work were not so conspicuously problematic as in her personal life, but they existed in abnormal abundance in the workplace as well.

In addition to the initial complaints at the outset of the therapy, two other important features emerged early. A sub-acute crisis existed with Jill's adolescent daughter who was acting out in school, at home, and socially. Although Jill was very angry with her misbehaving daughter, the anger really arose from the inconvenience that the girl's actions created for Jill. The daughter was obviously the designated patient in a family neurosis. The second initial feature was Jill's terrible sustained fear of death.

In the course of the psychotherapy, Jill was always an example of remarkable contradictions. On one hand she presented himself as an aggressive and effective creative executive, yet she would shamelessly express her multiple fears, accompanied by loud pleas to be relieved of her pain and guided in the right direction. She told me that our sessions were supposed to help her have a love affair with an extraordinarily handsome and accomplished man, but I focused more actively on the problems with her daughter. It was apparent that in her family Jill was living a lie, pretending to be a mother, while in fact reacting to her daughter as an inconvenient distraction from her narcissistic search for love from a sadistic father and a missing mother. I believe that my approach meant to Jill that I understood her need for effective parenting instead of being tricked by her into trying to relieve the anxiety du jour. I interpreted her search for narcissistic satisfaction as the futile search for the good parents outside herself, while the battle raged within. I always felt that Jill was basically a strongly motivated patient, but she maintained distance from me by her reluctance to discuss interpretations that connected present with past or that dealt with the therapeutic relationship as relevant to her life problems.

In conducting the therapy, I have consistently taken a listening, non-critical, interpretive stance, punctuated by reassurance and advice in emotionally or realistically urgent situations. For years, Jill's capacity for free association, taking in interpretation, and remembering dreams was extremely limited. My function seemed to be substitutive and supportive. The status quo was frustrating for me: I felt that Jill could let me be close to her only in ways that she rigorously controlled. By managing the therapeutic intimacy in this way, she inadvertently revealed her lying tendencies in intimacy: she lied to protect her fragile self; she did not dare to be truthful because of a profound and unalterable belief that truthful self- revelation would be ruthlessly exploited by her narcissistically exploitative father.

In an early session Jill explained her attitude to me: she needed to know that I was reliably there but not close. With an outstretched stiff arm, she showed how she kept me at a safe distance. But simultaneously she closed her fist as though clutching me tightly so that I could not abandon her. Safety rather than intimacy characterized the analysis as well as the rest of her life. In a strange way I felt used, objectified, and unloved through much of the therapy. Similarly, I could feel a certain coldness toward Jill. Recurringly, her pleasant or desperate demeanor could suddenly become imperiously hostile. This too had to be seen as part of her narcissistic defensiveness. She never took the opportunity to examine the roots of this kind of socially cruel behavior. If she became displeased by some imperfection in the other person, her own behavior seemed to her to be appropriate to the offense because this flaw in the other person jeopardized Jill's emotional safety. There was no apparent thought that she might have hurt the other person's feelings and that an apology might be in order. It also appeared that after the incident there was no further thought given to the event, no interest in reflection that might have been useful in the therapy. Insight was a mildly interesting bit of arcana, but not of value, or so she thought, in making herself feel good right now!

Jill was suffering with a serious deficit of loving experience, because of the severe strictures in loving that were bequeathed by her parents, primarily her father, and secondarily her mother. She could not provide love effectively—to others or herself. She knew the sensation of love but was incapable of living it. She could not absorb it, nor could she give it to others. Thus, she acquired a false self instead of an authentic loving self. Graphically, one might perceive her presenting self as a hollow shell. The deficit of fluent loving made it imperative that she develop stringent measures to protect her fragile self from dissolution. The shell-like self carefully regulated input from others and prevented any satisfying spontaneous expressiveness; instead, it enabled her to control her interaction with others so that she minimized her risk.

All the while, Jill's anxiety, rage, and guilt proliferated dangerously in their confinement. Her relationships predominantly involved self-protection, stealing a march, calculation of the odds of acceptance or rejection, and various similar maneuvers singularly lacking affectionate, trusting, or sentimental quality. The conspicuous absence of loving intentions and efforts was necessary for the relentlessly efficient manipulation of the human environment, but her stifled and stunted authentic loving self suffered. The obviously narcissistic anxiety, rage, and depression that Jill endured did, however, contain the "healthy" pain of a rudimentary trapped loving self. Jill's pathological narcissistic defenses were gradually weakened. This slowly liberated her loving potentials.

The Exhausting Effort to Support the False Self

Jill's power-oriented false self was antithetical to her authentic loving self. Domination and control are the hallmarks of the false self, and lying in various forms is the most effective way to promote and protect the false self. The devastating impact of this false self-preserving technique on relational processes must be recognized. What I began to realize at an early date in our work was that my expectations of Jill's mutative response to my interventions would be dashed. This generated painful reactions in me: I knew that I was useful, but in a very impersonal and undifferentiated way. Many evidences of disdain, contempt, doubt, and indifference toward me recurred, but usually were never expressed directly. These negating sentiments were embedded in the process, so they were felt powerfully by me, but were designed to elude effective interpretation. Her chronic lateness, frequent cancellations, and numerous absences for out-of-town trips also eroded my optimal therapeutic need to be open and emotionally available. Through all this it seemed futile to interpret because the ideas offered had no apparent meaning or interest to her, and they engendered no discernible change.

The supreme expression of her neurotic pattern was her search for an ideal love with a man outside the marriage. Early in the therapy, she began a long affair. Obviously, she was avoiding her marital relationship, and I made numerous interpretations about this reason for seeking the affair. I always sensed also that she was deflecting feeling from the therapy into her affair, but only much later in the therapy did it become possible to get her to focus on this displacement from the therapy.

After ten years of therapy, Jill made a firm decision that this would be the year during which she would terminate her firmly established policy of lying her way through her personal life. For the preceding decade, she had led a double life, lying to both her husband and her boyfriend. She concealed her extra-marital relationship from her husband essentially by falsifying the nature of her numerous trips outside of Los Angeles. She repeatedly told her lover that she'd left her husband or that she would soon do so—but neither of these assertions was true.

During the first nine years of therapy, Jill was remarkably refractory to fluent collaboration in the analytic dialogue. For instance, interpretations of general resistance seemed to go unheard; interpretations of transference were apparently ineffectual. Past-present interpretations were accepted by her as intellectually interesting and probably true but of no evident evocative or mutative influence. She exulted when she gained power—in any form. She suffered intensely when there was a reduction of power—in any form.

All the while, the strains arising from the deceits in her personal life and the manipulations in her occupational life steadily sapped her strength and confidence. She often appeared haggard and disheveled, and her comportment with her husband was distant and robotic. Whereas previously, she would pay lip service to conjoint therapy to restore meaning to her marriage, she now made no mention of the subject. Simultaneously, she became increasingly paranoid about her boyfriend—convinced that he was betraying her sexually. She employed devious and dishonorable methods as she attempted to confirm her suspicions. Although she understood intellectually that she was thereby managing her own neurotic distrust and guilt, these obvious meanings had no evident effect on her inappropriate beliefs and behaviors.

These egregious reactions crescendo-ed during the ninth year. Retrospectively, it would appear that during the near-decade a healthy self had gradually been growing in the benign and empathic therapeutic atmosphere. Thus, the neurotic frenzy constituted a final and futile effort to thwart the underlying actualization of a loving and honest self. As the year ended, Jill resolved that she would normalize her life during the forthcoming year. This meant that she would make a genuine decision, either to leave her marriage and commit to an honest and faithful relationship with her lover, or to tell the boyfriend truthfully that she intended to work seriously on improving her marriage and was therefore ending their relationship.

The very fact that Jill made this important and unprecedented announcement of intention indicated to me that her self had gradually undergone enormous submerged expansion and actualization during the previous years of analysis.

These crucial changes beg for elaborated explanation as follows: In every therapeutic relationship, a deep, complex, and decisive interaction unfolds that inexorably influences the manifest aspects of the therapy. Early in our interactions I intuited Jill's need for a warm and trustworthy father, and the firmly felt presence of a mother—and I therefore sensed that these provisions were required from me.

It therefore became crucial that my complicated relationship issues with my mother and father be mobilized unconsciously. My loving attitudes to Jill were not only necessary substitutive maternal and paternal offerings; I was also unconsciously identifying with her and living out my own lingering similar unmet needs. Jill feared these invitations to intimacy and rejected me with her imperious narcissism. When I then subtly recoiled with coldness and austerity, it was due to my own childish hurt. At the same time, my coldness represented the emotionally deprived parent in me.

As Jill and I repeated this nuclear engagement week after month after year, we both underwent gradual change in our underlying frightened, angry, guilty little child selves. When Jill's narcissistic defenses subsided within our relationship, I was simultaneously changing—my defense of aloof withdrawal had also diminished. Each of us was meeting a changed person.

This impingement and interpenetration of salient relational themes of both patient and therapist regularly results in both parties during the course of therapy and produces needed change, primarily in the patient but also in the therapist. The previously hidden and paralyzed loving father and mother become released within the patient—also, but subordinated, in the therapist.

Now Jill began participating in the therapy in drastically more effective ways. These included receptiveness to interpretation, richer quality of free association, dedication to maintaining our appointment schedule (re. cancellation and punctuality), remembering dreams, willingness to examine her narcissistically determined attitudes to me, and readiness to appreciate the role of internalized relations in the construction of current life experience—including the therapeutic relationship. These changes all represented major accretions of truthfulness in her psychological life, in contrast to the prior defensive patterns.

Jill's therapeutic behavior became more satisfying to us both. The relative profusion of thematically complex and pertinent dreams provided us with rich material for discussion. The waking correlate of these dreams was Jill's increasing ability and readiness for the first time, to connect her tangled love relationships, her developmental crises, and her powerful but largely un-elucidated involvement with me.

Heralding these fateful developments was the following dream:

"I am in an office up high. I see a terrible storm. The waves rise so high they look as though they are coming to the top. Others there don't seem to know or care. I am horrified that the waves will engulf the building."

This oceanic prelude to the ensuing tumultuous year contained various interpenetrating meanings that rose with terrifying wave-like power from the deep storminess of Jill's inner world to my therapeutic office, situated high, dry, and presumably safe, near the top of a tall building. She was now able to begin to explore the turbulence of her psychological world, rather than persisting interminably in her traditional defensive enactments (most importantly her avoidance of dangerous intimate commitment by leading a complex double life).

One month later Jill dreamed:

"My boyfriend is in Europe, and I am here. I look through the address book of an old female friend of mine, and I find my lover's European phone number. I hadn't even realized that he was betraying me."

At the time of this dream, Jill had not yet pronounced unequivocally that she would make a decision about commitment during this year. She was still experiencing massive, developmentally primitive distrust. During the year, it was she, not he, who stringently avoided commitment and who nevertheless maintained consistent distrust of him. Over the years of my work with Jill, I always felt that her sexual adventures in part expressed concealed eroticized attitudes of betrayal and deceit. Her rigidly clinging behavior with me and her aversion to deep association, while simultaneously maintaining diffusely suspicious attitudes toward others—particularly the lover—reinforced my sense that she compulsively lived out paranoid transference potentials to me that were too frightening for her to face directly.

Why would this sophisticated, worldly, intellectually developed and sensitive woman approach the therapeutic task with such seeming superficiality? Her early announcement that I was austere was a profound, if obscure, disclosure. She warned me that it was not safe to trust her, and simultaneously she perceived that my potential for guardedness was immediately mobilized in her byzantine presence. She certainly entertained and charmed me, but she could never allow an engagement suffused with mutual trust, acceptance, and vulnerability. I discovered, repeatedly, that whenever I began to believe in her and relaxed my professional distance—at any time that she felt narcissistically threatened—she would become arrogantly critical and dismissive, with no apparent concern for my sensibilities. In these periods, she had no tolerance for human frailty—except her own. It is true that she also enjoyed reading my thoughts and opinions, knowing what my next comments, even silent ones, would be. This intimate interpenetration of minds could be abruptly truncated by any downward turn in Jill's narcissistic fortunes, and the contemptuously devaluing comments predictably emerged—reintroducing active, mutually suspicious sentiments to the inter-subjective field. Jill acknowledged that her impressive ability to understand other people was accompanied by a singular lack of reliable empathy.

Jill's "justifiable paranoia" can be construed as an understandable adaptive response to the prison-like atmosphere of her childhood home. Her father successfully maintained a reign of terror for many years. She watched as he contemptuously drove her mother into depressive withdrawal, treating her as a weak, useless drone. Similarly, she saw him demonize and engage in verbal battle with her sister. Since the king-father anointed Jill the little princess, she safely watched from the sidelines as this ugly scene was enacted day after day.

This dream of betrayal by her boyfriend and her female friend condenses Jill's myriad historical and contemporary relational symptomatic issues. These important themes were elaborated, as in the preceding paragraphs, during the next number of weeks in the therapeutic dialogue. As the preoccupation with betrayal was alleviated, Jill's feelings for me erupted through the following dream:

"I am in Iraq, walking in a public square. I come upon a woman being whipped in an unusual way: she is lying on her back with her legs pulled up. They are whipping her. Then they stop whipping. The woman isn't crying. Then the woman is standing, dressed, with a small disc-shaped lump on her right cheek. The woman is holding the hand of a little girl."

As we explored this dream, it appeared that, with the reduction of the eroticized distrustful fascination with the father, an accompanying unconscious masochistic yearning for the mother gained some ascendancy—the beating being capped by the final moment of woman and girl holding hands. This newfound, ambivalent intimacy with her mother was now expressed in the greater openness she was now enjoying with me. She offered herself more readily to my interpretations, which were often experienced by her as both stinging and stimulating, as in the dream of being whipped. As she repeatedly reconfirmed her intention to end the affair during this year, she was realizing that her masochistic yearning for love from her mother was an attempt to find a loving alternative to her terrifying father. She was also realizing that the painful yearning for her father persisted. The drastic current reduction of defensiveness with me was enabling more profoundly intimate communication to occur between us.

As though released by the recognition of her painful longing for her mother (therapist), Jill followed up with three intimate but troubled dreams about her father, sister, and mother:

1. "I am in bed. A man gets in and puts his leg next to mine. It's my father. I'm shocked. He says, 'If you don't love me, I will die.' I scream, 'I can't handle it.' Then I am with my husband, and scream to him about what my father did. My husband says, 'Keep it quiet, don't scream.'"

2. "I am outside my childhood home. I lay my head on the car

roof and I am crying because I haven't visited my grandmother. My boyfriend asks why I'm crying, and my sister says that my grandmother is dead."

3. "I am on a subway or bus, perhaps with my husband. Someone is a homemaker. I ask if she knew my mother. I get off and start to cry. My mother was known, she had a presence, she touched some lives. It was deeply moving."

This triad of dreams bears Jill's inimitable imprimatur. Her seductive, menacing, guilt-evoking father displays his aggressive wares. Jill is horrified, but she submits to the instructions of her husband, to whom she has assigned paternal surrogacy. In consequence, as in the second dream, she can only long sadly for the lost grandmother, the only loving female relation permitted to Jill by her father during her childhood. Finally, in the third dream, Jill can experience the previously forbidden mother love. Jill could appreciate that the increasing exposure of the meanings of her father's controlling behavior and her bitter distance from her mother was reflected in a drastic shift in the transference. That is, she was now relaxing her frozen, distancing grip on me, as though I was no longer the omnipotent, invasive but desperately needed father. Instead, she was experiencing tender, receptive feelings toward me through which she now enjoyed interpretations as comforting and strengthening, as from a lovingly available mother.

At the same time that Jill could absorb and respond to interpretation, she achieved a stunning realization that she, like all of us, consists of the totality of both her parents—the bad as well as the good. This became more than acceptance; she could now embrace, even love, these diverse qualities in herself. And thus she could enjoy a major expansion of her loving self. This expanded relational capability became a force in the liberation of the loving self.

Throughout this period of important work during the first several months of 2003, Jill's transformative immersion in the therapeutic process was satisfying to both of us. It meant that she could surrender to intimacy, that she could eventually become able to commit to a love relationship, and that she could live through love, rather than survive (perilously) through lies.

As these welcome insights and relational shifts were absorbed and consolidated over subsequent weeks, Jill rose to the challenge of new relational strength. The result was a remarkable dream with epiphanic power:

"I go to a room—to make love to my lover. He is naked but covered. Two women stand, one on either side of him. I know I am supposed to go down on him. But as I suck, I resent the coercion."

Jill appreciated readily that this dream portrayed the leitmotif of her family, and she emphasized that she now realized that there were three other females and one male in her family of origin. Why, she asked, did she never realize this gender distribution? Why did she always assume there were no women in the family other than herself? This was true even though she always knew she had a mother and a sister.

The dream was readily decodable by Jill. She realized that her lover is really the king-father. The mother and sister are like servants, standing on duty beside the king-father. He is the phallic father who requires eroticized phallic worship from Jill. He anoints her, she enjoys his favors, but she loses her self. In consequence, she constructs a false self in something like the following manner: the germinal true self of the little girl is stifled by the absence of a loving and encouraging inter-subjective climate because of the father's own obsession with power. Jill, as the anointed princess, learns that control and domination are essential for survival, and lying becomes central to her interpersonal experience. So Jill's life became a series of survival crises, requiring desperately manipulative measures.

Releasing the Loving Self

A loving, trusting, truth-telling self promotes a relational climate of confidence, constructive energy, and safety. While the potential for such self functions existed for Jill, these could never become actualized. Her paradigmatic dream of sucking the man's penis exposed her driving concept of human relations: everything is a function of domination and submission. But being able to have the dream, and to participate in interpretive discussion of it, was itself indicative of Jill's newly emerging loving self.

In her previous self-state, Jill was riddled with somatic fears, including fear of death. She fluctuated between narcissistic grandiosity and narcissistic despair. And of course she could not commit. To have done so would have entailed making herself vulnerable and thereby inviting destruction by some powerful other. In contrast, as the true self was becoming ascendant, these fears and fluctuations receded remarkably, because Jill was withdrawing from her favored but perilous status in the court of the absolute monarch.

The precursor endangered self, traumatized by the implacably dominating father, had to eschew honest self-expression. Instead, the self had no choice but to please the father, that is, to appease him, sacrificing honest spontaneity. The loving self, stunted and sequestered, finally emerged from hiding. In this process, it filled the previously empty expanse of the false self.

9.

From Cloistered Self to Loving Self: A View from Within

When the circumstances of early family life make it perilous for a child to express an exuberant zest for life in a confident and secure way, one alternative is a subdued, austere, vigilant, and constricted approach to life. This is the cloistered self in action.

A woman in her forties came to me because of her powerful involvement with her angry, controlling, self-righteous, and depriving father. She was living an ascetic, withdrawn, and colorless life at the outset of our work.

In addition to the inherently instructive value of this case, an unusual document was written by the patient, whom I will call Mona, in which she reveals her analysis of her therapy with me. This carefully composed additional perspective on our work, included herein, enriches our comprehensive understanding of how this patient's stifled loving self ultimately and ecstatically prevailed.

My work with the patient consisted of enabling an extremely inhibited youngish woman to open up to the world of relationships and achieve loving fulfillment. Due in part to our difference in age, the therapy could be framed as a kind of father-daughter relationship, in which her experience with me effectively enabled the release of her loving self from its father-based constriction.

The Self Goes Into Hiding

Mona is the older of two children born to Jewish parents from New York. The father came from a gangster family, involved in typical racketeering, the mother's family was more conventional. Both parents were moderately active leftists, with the father standing out as the family lightening rod, regularly drawing attention to himself. The mother, for the most part, deferred to her husband. She was much gentler, but less charismatic and compelling. Early in her life, Mona adored and revered her father. Later on, she detested him. In either regard, the father was always the central figure of Mona's family involvement.

When she was a young child, Mona had to endure her father's tantrum-like eruptions of rage. He was a writer who wrote at home, always controlling the activity in the family's relatively small living space. Mona's brother, her only sibling, was prone to similar tantrums and eruptions during childhood, and grew into a socially inhibited and withdrawn adult.

Everyone in the family was involved in analytically oriented psychotherapy. Mona was in therapy for years during her childhood, when her family lived in constant dread of punitive authority because of their political interests. In the 1950s, during the McCarthy era, the family had to be prepared to go into hiding or exile at an instant's notice. This very real danger terrified Mona and contributed to her social isolation. My own similar left-wing background, with the same fears and apprehensions, was an important component of the reciprocally empathic bridge we established. It may be that the political threat was also an exterior organizing focus for the intra-familial relational dreads. Throughout this trying youth, Mona performed brilliantly in the private schools she attended, as well as the Ivy League University in which she eventually enrolled.

Mona began seeing me when her female therapist of many years retired from practice. Mona was working as a lawyer in a firm where she had no hope of becoming a partner. Also at that time, she was in the process of ending a decade-long relationship with a man who had social and intimate inhibitions similar to her own. Except for her six or more cats, she lived alone in an apartment with virtually no furnishings. Mona spoke almost in a whisper, and dressed severely in somber-colored clothing that exposed only her head, hands, and lower legs.

70

I saw her as a secular nun; or, perhaps more accurately, as a fervent cat worshipper who had fashioned her own solipsistic religion. From the start of our collaboration, I realized that she needed to open up—to move into the relational world, and let that world enter her life. One useful indicator of progress as our work advanced was the diminishing number of cats she doted on.

Other important changes that occurred during Mona's therapy were the development of a stronger speaking voice; her freedom to dress herself in more feminine and colorful ways; her growing interest in furnishings and decorating her home; the decision to rid herself of her cats; and the shift in her career to a more satisfying law specialty. The culmination of these changes came when Mona met a woman with whom she fell in love, and then married. To provide some idea of how profoundly her loving self had been stifled, I had no conception that Mona had lesbian potentials until the day that she announced to me that she had fallen in love with a woman.

Why do different types of false self occur? Why did Mona develop a cloistered self rather than a distracted or a lying self? To start with, Mona grew out of a secretive, apprehensive family, who symbolically huddled together in fear of the menacing political winds. This factor should be neither underestimated nor exaggerated. More than this, Mona's father was a cloistered man (a cloistered self) with a distinctly paranoid sense that others were mistreating him. At the same time, he blindly elicited their rejecting responses. He controlled Mona's social and play activities to an inordinate degree, prohibiting, for instance, modest and safe unsupervised neighborhood pastimes, such as riding her bike around the block. Along with his excessive restraints, he promoted in his daughter an idolatrous attitude toward him. This lasted until late adolescence, when Mona's unswerving idealization of her father gradually died and was replaced by bitterness and contempt. Simultaneously, her longstanding belief that her mother was an inferior impediment was transformed into modest affectionate respect for her mother's steadfast capacity to absorb her father's domineering self-righteousness, all for the sake of preserving the family.

In the course of her therapy, the relationships with her father, mother, and brother were each intensively revisited. In all instances, the residual negative sentiments that had dominated her underlying attitudes were gradually restored to a suitably subordinated position. Resigned affection replaced her previous irritable impatience with her father. Similarly, the former admixture of pity and disappointment toward her mother receded as Mona replaced her condescending attitude with more lovingly intense feelings.

As a result, Mona lost the almost superhuman estimation of her father she had formed early in life. Without denying he'd done considerable damage to all family members, not least himself, Mona was now able to see her father as fallible, but deserving respect for his ferocious devotion to his family. Furthermore, she was able to appreciate that her father had achieved little more than a successful career as a journeyman screenwriter, who might have been more creative had he not obstructed himself with his own self-damaging eccentricities.

The Therapeutic Bridge

Because of our shared socio-political background and our similar current socio-cultural views, I knew Mona experienced me and my active verbal engagement with her as different from her previous therapists. She welcomed my refusal to accept her massively inhibited status quo. As a result, we were able to maintain an intense, serious, but playful dialogical process.

As our therapeutic intimacy unfolded, I had a very illuminating experience. In one session, as I looked at Mona's face, I saw the face of my eldest sister, who was an auxiliary mother figure for me. This visual hallucination lasted for a few minutes, until I decided to erase it. This experience revealed my intense sister-mother involvement with Mona, including dependent, ambivalent, and erotic elements. I believe Mona sensed this intense subjective impingement, and it enabled her to focus on her father-daughter preoccupation in our therapeutic interaction. She was able to engage in a relationship with me that was quite different from the one she had had with her defensively controlling father. Ultimately, as she appreciated my unconcealed vulnerability to the female, Mona could more safely discover the gently loving father she needed as a child and as an adult.

At a turning point, several years later in the therapy, Mona had a counterpart waking hallucination. As she described it, it took place in her home where she lives happily with her wife. Her dead father appeared, alive and positive. He was approving of her, her home, and her adult life.

They felt loving toward each other. Then, she let him go.

By demonstrating a crucial transformation of the hapless, thwarting entrapment of her early father experience and the consequent relational isolation it imposed on her life, this fantasy confirms the ultimately successful release of Mona's previously confined and unrecognized loving self.

After almost a decade of working together, I asked Mona if she would be willing to write something about how she perceived her therapy, and how it liberated her. I informed her that I would use her document for teaching purposes and that others would read it. This is her account:

Three Dreams and Two Poems

I started with Joe in 1998. I was stiff, anxious, and untrusting, although I don't think I would have described myself that way at the time. I'm not Catholic, but Joe told me later that I behaved like an austere nun. He wasn't the first to tell me this.

My struggle was with my father, a man whose early life was so baroquely bizarre and so profoundly painful that he should have grown up to be an axe murderer. I've always admired him for having been brave, even though he was fundamentally fearful, especially during the blacklist years of the 1950s and early 1960s.

My father was at his best with animals and very small children, with whom he did not have to negotiate the clumsy and hurtful problems of separation and interdependence. We had lots of cats all through my childhood, and my father adored them. When I was a child, he adored me, too. He entered my life so completely that I became the guardian of his happiness. I knew even as a small child that I understood him better than my mother did, that I alone could deeply reassure him that all was well in his life, that I alone could see his rage about to burst and could cause his swelling fury to dissipate.

I worshipped my father. He was a terribly fragile man, and my heart broke for his fragility. He was a terrifyingly angry man, but even in my twenties I was convinced that a different person spoke from his body when he was angry. I felt that I had great authority within our family because he was mine in a way that he was not my mother's. My brother was an angry boy; my father was an angry man; my mother was ineffectual with both of them. It was up to me to preserve the family by preventing my father from becoming angry. It was up to me to be the good child and maintain the balance in our family between people who had temper tantrums and people who didn't. A ratio of two people who had tantrums to two who didn't meant that the family was balanced, even if it wasn't happy. If I turned, the ratio would slide: with three people who had temper tantrums, the family would be destroyed.

When I started to see Joe, I wanted to be free of my father. He had been dead for several years (he died on my birthday, of galloping lung cancer, and I sometimes thought that he chose that day to die just so that I would never be free of him), but he had a terrifying life within me. I described us to Joe as Greco-Roman Wrestlers, each tightly gripping the other in a constricting hold, neither able to throw the other off, neither willing to let the other win, locked implacably together, muscles frozen. I had had dreams all my life about being chased by people who wanted to kill me, and we decided fairly early on that the murderous pursuers in all of those dreams were my father. A few years into the therapy, I was still having those dreams of homicidal pursuit, including this disturbing variation:

I'm alone in my parents' house. I'm in the kitchen when I realize that my father has come home. He is carrying two brown paper grocery bags, one in each hand. When he sees me, his face contorts with murderous fury and he rushes towards me, the bags still hanging from his hands. I am certain that he intends to kill me.

No longer masked as an anonymous maniac, or a prison guard, or Nazi, there was my father. I'd been seeing Joe for a while, which perhaps explains the telling grocery bags. My father did provide for us. Or did they represent my abandonment, my withdrawal of love? Either way, he wanted to kill me.

I wanted to be free of my father. I was like him in ways that repelled me. I felt him embedded inside me, and I told Joe that I wanted to amputate him. I didn't like hearing that I couldn't, and I liked even less Joe's assurance that what I must do was learn to cuddle up to my father in me. Cuddle up to the dragon at the end of the sofa? I didn't want to, and I didn't believe Joe when he said that it was both possible and desirable. What I wanted was expressed in the first of the two poems in this piece. The poem is "O Where Are You Going?" by W.H. Auden. In the poem, reader asks rider where he is going; fearer asks farer whether he really thinks that his "diligent looking" will find the right road; horror asks hearer about the silent, soft figures sinisterly, swiftly following behind. This is the last stanza:

> "Out of this house"—said rider to reader,
> "Yours never will"—said farer to fearer,
> "They're looking for you"—said fearer to horror,
>   As he left them there, as he left them there.

(I just opened my edition of Auden's collected poems to check the punctuation and saw, startled, an inscription to my father written by my father: "To W., from His Worst Enemy—W.")

The Terrible Effort to Conceal the Loving Self

I knew most of what I've just written about my father by the time I began with Joe. What I didn't know was the immensity of the effort I was making to keep my father in his place. I mean that phrase in every respect. I was guarded and tense because I knew that I was like him in ways that I despised; if I couldn't get rid of him, then I would make his place in me a bare and cheerless corner, and try to keep him there. On the other hand, I was living in a large apartment with nothing but a mattress on the floor, forty boxes of books, a desk and a chair, and six cats. Clearly, a meaningful love life was out of the question; my father, represented by the cats he adored, had primacy of place. I was living in my own life a version of the paranoid isolation that my father had lived in his; I worshiped my cats as I had worshiped him.

Joe has asked me to write this piece about how I got from where I was to where I am now. I'm glad he asked, because I'm tired of reading papers he's written about patients who aren't me; but I don't know how to describe what's happened to me. A friend of mine commented recently that I'd done a lot of work with Joe, and I appreciate that she recognizes how much I've changed; but it hasn't felt like work. It's felt like the opposite of work. Work is, for me, linear; this has felt diffuse and impressionistic. Work means effort, determination, and a fairly high level of bureaucratic diplomacy; but I don't feel that I've marshaled my forces, girded my loins, or conducted strategic negotiations. It's been the opposite of that: not grimness, but lightness; not effort, but enjoyment; not war or even parade rest, but armistice and amnesty. I've read some of Joe's papers and am familiar with some of his theories, but I find theory, even his theory, uncongenial and remote. I can't connect it except with great effort, and in the most distant way, to my interior and exterior life.

All I can say is that my father became an ordinary man. He even shrank physically in my mind from immensity to his true, ordinary size. I grew to see him as a man—just a man. He was born in a particular year, and he was bounded by the places in which he grew and the times in which he lived. He was talented in his field, but he was no genius, and his work now looks dated, because time and taste have moved on.

I don't know how my father became ordinary. I knew the outlines of my life before my therapy began. I don't know how that wrestler's death grip relaxed; but it did, first mine, then my father's. I even offered my hand to my father as I stood up on the wrestling mat and stretched my cramped muscles. How did that happen? Joe is a father, and is about the age my father would be if he were alive. I felt daughterly toward him and I know I've acted that way, and in the process, my notions of my father as a father, and of myself as a daughter, softened and relaxed. I don't know how it happened. Joe and I just talked, and I used to cry. In fact, for quite a while I rated my sessions by how much I had cried, a Kleenex Index. But the Kleenex Index slumped to nothing quite a while ago, and now it doesn't seem to matter.

Around the time my father became ordinary, three or four years into the therapy with Joe, I fell in love. I had told Joe a few years earlier that I was worried about falling on love: It would mean displacing him as the most important person in my life. I think that he said that our relationship would change but wouldn't suffer. I didn't believe him, of course, but he was right. He is important to me in a way that M. is not, and M. is certainly important to me in a way that Joe is not. My hierarchy has dissolved.

Also, I became massively allergic to cats. If it hadn't hurt so much, I'd have thought it was funny. M. sympathized, but, no animal lover, she secretly rejoiced. I've wondered whether I would have developed so crippling an allergy if I'd had a different father, or a different lover, or a different therapist. M. and I bought a house together, and I found other homes for my cats. I noticed after the last two had gone how much more energy I had. I really was surprised, and I still don't know whether to attribute my vitality to the decline of cat worship in its emotional or its physical form. I suppose there's no need to choose one or the other.

A year or so after M. and I moved into our house, I had a dream, which wasn't really a dream, because I wasn't asleep or even in bed. I was standing in my living room. It was night. M. was asleep in our bedroom downstairs, but I was working late. I had taken a little break from my work, and my father appeared. He wasn't exuberant or even demonstrably pleased to see me. He was calm, and, for him, relaxed. What was most remarkable about his appearance that night (the fact of his appearance did not seem remarkable at all) was that he was, mostly, relating to me as if I were a person who was his daughter, instead of his daughter who, as he might or, more probably, might not from time to time remember, was also a separate person.

He looked around the room and asked if this was where I lived, and I told him it was. In a slight expression of his habitual anxiety, he asked if the neighborhood was safe, and I said that it was very quiet. I showed him the living room in the dim light from the street, and the dining room, and the kitchen and guestroom. I took him up the ladder from the guestroom to my tiny study in the attic. He asked if my mother had been up there, and I told him that she had a bad knee now that kept her off the ladder, but that I was considering making her a periscope. He saw a photo of M. and asked who it was. I told him how much we love each other and how happy we are together. He nodded, taking it in. I asked if it hurt to be dead. He smiled a small smile and said no, it didn't. I don't think we had more conversation—Joe's notes will be more complete; but this is what I remember. We simply stayed in a state of mutual recognition. I felt him puzzled about my living in this house with M.—a little hurt by it perhaps (it meant that I had left him), and a little bit triumphant to be in a room that my mother, who after all was still alive, had not been able to enter.

I don't remember my father disappearing, and it wasn't anything sudden. I think that, after a time, I just nodded and smiled a little and turned back to my work.

I don't know what more to say. I see Joe twice a week and we talk. M. and I are planning our wedding. I'm closer to my brother. I can spend an entire weekend with my mother without hating her for her immaturity. I want my mother and my brother to see me get married, even though my brother will behave strangely and my mother will get drunk and try to make herself the center of attention. We're just an ordinary family.

My father is a presence in my life, but not all the time, and never overwhelmingly. I've noticed that I comment fairly often to friends these days, wryly or lovingly, "My dad used to say...." I've become an ordinary person.

Dream: There's been some sort of natural disaster, but very localized—confined, in fact, to the house in which M. and I are living. (It's not the house that we actually live in, but a much taller one with a basement.) I am barred from entering because the structure is unstable. After some hours, though, I'm escorted inside by a volunteer first responder to salvage what I can. I realize how unprepared I am: I unthinkingly try to flick on the lights before realizing that the power is of course out. Rubble is everywhere, and dirty dust is thick on every surface. I try to think what to save. Books, papers, perhaps jewelry? But everything is equally valuable and therefore equally valueless. I'll leave it all. I walk carefully downstairs into the basement. My flashlight casts a feeble yellow light on the dust, the rubble, the meaningless objects beneath. No, I'm not going to take anything. Then I feel a thunderbolt of guilt: the cats, the cats, how can I have forgotten them? Are they hiding, terrified, in this house that is now on the brink of collapse, or have they fled in fear? Are they wounded in the debris? How can I have forgotten my cats? Then, just as suddenly, I shake myself and calm returns—I don't have cats anymore, they're long gone from here, they're all safe. So what shall I take from the ruins of this house? Nothing. Everything here has equal value and thus, no value. They're just things. I don't need any of them.

So Joe, my first responder, helped me tour the fallen temple of cat worship. The actual house where I grew up did have a basement. I pass within a block of it early every Tuesday morning, driving to my appointment with Joe. I once told Joe in a moment of bitter anger that I needed a fireman and I had in him only an archaeologist. In this dream, he is both.

The second poem of this piece is a few lines from a sonnet by Gerard Manley Hopkins titled "Hurrahing the Harvest," in which the poet, with his characteristic ecstatic exactitude, describes the beauty of a harvest field. He ends with this propulsive observation:

These things, these things were here, and but the beholder
Wanting; which two when they once meet,
The heart rears wings bold and bolder

And hurls for him, O half hurls earth from him off under his feet.

Also, I'll leave it to Joe to talk about how this poem describes therapy from the analyst's point of view, but I can say that my work with Joe made my heart rear wings. I became able to love M. and my father and myself. My dreams are, sadly, far more plodding and prosaic than Hopkins' marvelous creations; he makes earth half hurl off under his feet, while I can only make a house teeter after an earthquake. Well, we have to accept at least some of our limitations. I'm not Hopkins, but the temple where I worshiped my father has turned to rubble, and I don't want to salvage anything. I still don't know how any of this happened, and in some respects I feel that trying to cram this experience into theory would distort and degrade it. I enjoy standing in the middle of it, surrounded, non-linear, amazed.

The Triumph of the Loving Self: Ecstatic Ordinariness

Mona's lyrical rendering of our therapeutic accomplishments happily proclaims, in every syllable, the triumph of the loving self. She has achieved ecstatic ordinariness; and it occurred not through labor, but through love. Or perhaps we should say that it was a labor of love. She hints at, but does not specify, the richly rewarding inter-subjective intimacy that we created. Out of this creation, we rescued and liberated her cloistered loving self. Yet Mona disclaims any need to understand how this happened. This paradoxical attitude really confirms our substantial achievement.

From the outset, it was painfully evident to me, as to any therapist, that Mona existed in a stifling cocoon of safety, without libidinal or assertive satisfaction. As we studied and separated the thousands of silken threads that had woven her into her cell, we could appreciate the marvelous tapestry of meanings that comprised her previously imprisoned inner self. So our dialogue became endlessly complex, pursuing filaments within the strands of fluctuating meaning. It is no wonder that Mona writes that she is satisfied to enjoy the rich results of our experience, leaving to me the explication of our process.

In a late therapy session, Mona began by emphasizing her affectionate experience with her wife during recent days—following several days of feeling verbally assaulted and invaded by her wife's incessant and insistent chatter. Mona also reported that she had recently had a profoundly intimate conversation with a dear female friend who was struggling to find a surrogate egg donor so that she and her husband might add a second child to their little family.

Mona then reported a dream: "I am on a train with my parents, being transported to a Nazi extermination camp. My father, helped by my mother, shoves me off the train to safety, while my parents go on to their grim fate."

Mona exclaimed that she had previously never dreamed of her father as self-sacrificing. But in the dream, he actively extruded her from the tight family circle of death that he, assisted by her mother, had created. Realizing that her dream expressed her inner world, she then understood that she was her father, transforming his previously perverse power into an act of self-liberation through which she was able to move into a life of autonomy, choice, and fulfillment.

A related feature of the session was Mona's report that, for the first time in her life, she had recently confronted and repudiated her mother's recurring invocation of her (mother's) oncoming death. She shouted her refusal at the mother, who reluctantly retracted the morbid reference. Mona felt empowered through this interaction. As in her dream, Mona chose active life over passive death. All these events confirm victory for Mona's loving self.

The Importance of Psychological Safety

This case is distinctive for one remarkable and compelling reason: throughout our long relationship, we enjoyed an unvarying freedom to understand and appreciate whatever the other said and thought (consciously and unconsciously). Hints and allusions (from either side of the relationship) were readily grasped with full awareness of the richness and specificity of all that was unsaid. The fact that she and I could each enjoy a happy hallucination of a family member within the context of our close dialogical relationship reveals the limitless safety we found in one another, vicariously fulfilling the thwarted hope of our respective developmental lives.

Of course, our inter-subjective engagement was not entirely symmetrical, inasmuch as she found an effective, but kind and gentle father in me, while I found loving sisters in her, for whom I could provide care, rather than vice-versa. The asymmetry was not only qualitative. From a quantitative standpoint, her inner and relational life changed much more than mine. But in the heart of the deep inter-subjective activity, asymmetry melts away, only to be restored as new relational balances are achieved. I think that our work was life changing for Mona, yet it was profoundly beneficial for me as well.

10.

The Ambivalence of the Loving Self:
Embrace of the Hated Other

The culminating event in the emancipation of the loving self occurs in the happy embrace of the deeply hated (and covertly loved) other. Acceptance that we are all ambivalent creatures is now virtually commonplace. Similarly, we now realize that true, pure love is a fictive assumption, resting perilously on what Phillips and Taylor call a sentimental, nostalgic view of love (or "kindness," as they label it).

Anger, hate, distrust, envy, contempt, and other negative elements constitute much of the self, loving or otherwise. And here let us name these negations—hate. The work of therapy enables the self to master the hate toward the other. This means relinquishing rationalization, denial, reversal, and defensive emulation, which are among the many ways that the individual remains blind, and thus preserves the problem.

No one can escape absorbing the parents into one's being, but the freed self becomes able to perceive, accept, welcome, even embrace and love these parts of the self—which have previously been only hated (consciously). Until the individual reaches this point, she has been unaware that the whole parent, including the resented aspects, was a fundamental part of herself, and so the distrust and bitterness toward the parent constituted a rejection of herself.

The Great Love Triangle

Since the experience of love is triadic (love of self, love of other, love from other), and since the love of the other requires acceptance of hateful aspects of the other, it necessarily includes awareness and acceptance of one's own hateful likeness to the other. The flaws of the other are my own flaws. I acknowledge, accept, welcome, embrace, and love these ignoble qualities (my own), which have previously been unacknowledged.

When a person loves all of herself, not just her grander elements, she is now freer to make more consistently loving and mature choices in life—she now enjoys emancipation of the loving self. The stifling of the loving self begins early in life, and the inevitable amnesia for our early years always clouds insight into the origins. As the therapeutic dialogue unfolds, the enlarging sensitivity in contemporary relationships permits increasingly reliable inferences about the shrouded past. Freud's emphasis on reconstruction in therapy has the same basis. As these past-present correlations accumulate, so does a continuing expansion of lovingly critical thinking about self and others.

The Hated Other(s)

Meg, a fiftyish matron, came to see me at her husband's insistence. He could no longer bear her criticisms of everything about him: clothing, eating habits, body appearance, aperitif preferences, conversational style, and on and on. Essentially, she entered therapy in response to an ultimatum.

Even though she entered therapy reluctantly, she was genuinely interested, but skeptical. She expected to be graded, hoping to receive high grades. She readily appreciated that the expectation of high grades in therapy derived from her relationship to her father; needing him to admire Meg at the expense of her mother and sister. She thought of her father as brighter than her mother or sister. But she also resented and feared the conditionality of his love. She enjoyed being father's favorite, but she felt her position was precarious. So she exalted her father, yet she felt a certain distaste toward him for not being handsome in her eyes.

In the early phase, I provided abundant support for her high intelligence and her expectations of high marks in therapy. She felt guiltily eager to impress her father; she dismissed her mother as a mediocrity; and she felt quite remote from her sister. I pointed out that she seemed to have no one in the family on whom she could feel safely dependent. And I suggested that she felt similarly distrustful toward her husband. Meg consciously yearned for him to make her happy by being warm and loving. But her hypercritical behavior elicited only bitterness and withdrawal. To make my point clear, I told her that she kept him on a leash with her controlling behavior, but this only made him more miserable and unloving.

She needed to let him go, because in her critical stance she was unconsciously living out earlier developmental issues. This combination of advice and interpretation was devoured, as though she felt safe to become dependent on me. She soon reported a major reduction in her narcissistic discontent with her husband. She was also becoming much closer to her sister. Her sister told Meg that she had spent years in therapy to overcome the pain that arose from Meg's rejection of her.

We agreed that in various ways Meg had rejected the three other members of her original family. I urged her to consider that in doing so she was repudiating herself, and that she needed to accept—even embrace—the resented and devalued others. Since she partook of all their qualities, embracing them meant loving and embracing herself—including her less loveable parts. I pointed out that learning to love these "hated" others meant that she could love their negative qualities as hers and in this way could more fully love herself, as well as all of the important people in her life.

Meg absorbed these interpretations without hesitation, and she made fundamental relational changes in her attitudes to her father, mother, and sister. Her husband also reported a quantum leap of gratification in their marital transactions. Her negative feelings toward family members, she now realized, included projections of her own angry self. In this manner, she had been defending her vulnerable self from the hazards of opening oneself to loving experience.

Previously, she had maintained a harshly judgmental attitude to her husband, contempt toward her mother, dismissive indifference to her sister, and ambivalent deference to her father. Her consciously resentful yearning for approval from her father pointed to his singular importance as the hated other. Her negations of husband, mother, and sister arose from her unconscious absorption of her father's similar judgmental and rejecting attitude. She drank in my interpretations involving the father in her and as her. She instantly understood the relieving value of embracing him in and as herself. No longer did she need to fend off this truth from herself. Her love for husband, mother, sister, and father could safely come out of hiding. This was another epiphany as described in the chapter on interpretation.

Hate and the Suppression of the Loving Self

This example illustrates the role of hate in the suppression of the loving self in the relational life of a neurotic woman who lives a life of civility and who grew up in a basically non-violent family with ample parental love that enabled her to develop a loving self. Her parents' neurotic traits, however, interfered with the free expression of her love. In a case such as this, the recognition of a parent's aggression in oneself can be very liberating.

The truth is that we are the hated other. In psychotherapy, this means that one is the hated parent. However, this truth has limits; it is relative. Its interpretation provides immense leverage—but only if the negating parental attitudes coexisted with abundant love. This combination fosters a loving self, but inhibits it at the same time. On the other hand, dangerous parents who inflict violently destructive attitudes and behaviors on the child prevent the development of a loving self in the child. Patients who have suffered this abuse may not derive benefit from the interpretation we are discussing. Instead, such patients need to discover the full range and intensity of their authentic fury to the parent(s).

Destructive parenting precludes the complex integration of loving and hating elements in the relational world of the victim-patient. Here, it is not valid or helpful to expect the patient to accept the virulent parent as oneself—in fact, the opposite is necessary: clearly establishing the fundamental difference between the virulent parent and oneself.

Embracing the Hated Other

The following case is another example of the importance of gaining insight into the ambivalence of the loving self in relation to the hated other.

Sophia, a fifty-year-old woman from Milan, was in psychotherapy because of persistent phobic reactions to all orthopedic and other medical devices. These symptoms had persisted since childhood. Two-and-a-half decades earlier she had had analytic therapy, because she suffered from anxiety and depression.

Sophia grew up in a tension-filled home. Her mother had severe leg deformity from poliomyelitis in childhood. So, the mother wore a leg brace. As Sophia grew, her mother became increasingly abusive and contemptuous toward Sophia's scholastic brilliance. She frequently gave Sophia the "silent treatment" for days, despite the youngster's desperate entreaties for affection and respect. Inevitably, by the time of adolescence, Sophia became very resentful, with associated guilt. Out of this troubled matrix, her phobic symptoms emerged.

Sophia recalled that when she began psychotherapy at age twenty-six, she told her therapist in the first session, "I want to reconcile with my mother before she dies." At age thirty, she met and married her American husband, moved to California, bore two children, and continued psychological training. Although she was relieved to achieve geographic distance from her mother, she felt considerable guilt over leaving, and consequently she felt socially insecure and neurotically sensitive to possible rejection by others.

More recently, the relationship with her mother had greatly improved; but the phobic symptoms remained, and so Sophia again sought therapy. Shortly thereafter, she reported the following dream:

"I am in Milan on holiday. I suddenly realize with panic that I have forgotten to tell my patients that I am on a trip, and I feel enormous guilt. I picture my patients waiting in my office, and I can feel their trust in me vanishing. I feel I have failed them and they will leave me. In order to bear the intense psychological pain, I tell myself, 'It is just a dream.' Then I awaken."

This dream represented a major turning point for Sophia. She made the following extremely cogent and useful observation about the dream: "The dream is the geographic reverse of my life experience in that I left Milan for Los Angeles in reality; but I left my needy mother in Milan just as I left my needy patients in the dream. The patients also portray my neediness (including my unconscious identification with my mother). I developed my assertive and achieving qualities as a defense against feeling handicapped and bitter like my mother; and I didn't realize that I had a needy side that required respect, protection, and care. Now, I appreciate a persistent split between my strong, self-sufficient side and my underlying weak, abandoned, and needy side."

Over recent years, Sophia's relationship to her mother has vastly improved. They enjoy a pleasant and close rapport. Sophia's dream indicated that the defensive split in her personality was healing. She has been able to appreciate how much she is like her wounded, angry, and vulnerable mother.

By embracing the hated qualities of her mother within herself Sophia has experienced an important consequent liberation and enlargement of her loving self. Furthermore, her chronic anxiety and persecutory feelings have dwindled. She remains a strongly assertive and goal-directed person, but these traits are no longer "ruling the show." She also points out that the thought, "It is just a dream," marks the emergence of the loving self.

And of course it should not surprise the reader that Sophia's phobic symptoms have vanished, as she now enjoys a sense of ease in the world.

The Objectifying Stance: A Barrier to the Loving Self

Most patients appreciate the complexity of their relationship to their parents. They realize that they possess deep love and also major negative feelings toward these same parents. They also realize, at least intuitively, that their inner world and their relational experience derive meanings and forms from their parents. This understanding, however, may be insufficient. That is, in their intimate relationships, they experience the rejections, controlling, betrayals, withholding by the other as objectively valid perceptions. Thus, these patients feel justified in controlling, resenting, repudiating, or otherwise attacking the other. With their objectifying stance, these patients are usually depriving themselves in two ways. First, they fail to see aspects of themselves (suffused with developmental relational meaning) in the objectionable features of the other. And second, this limitation of full awareness of their own unacceptable qualities arises from sequestration of ambivalent aspects of the self, which means that liberation of self qualities (including the loving self) is incomplete, and loving experience is correspondingly depleted.

The above circumstance is the usual one. The patient is unaware of the identification with the family member. However, the therapist optimally maintains a background awareness, as a distinct aspect of her general sustained awareness of the patient's continuous transferential involvement. The unique aspect here is the patient's fear of becoming aware that the disliked elements of the parental other are really also parts of the self that represent negative features of the parent that have been absorbed into and constitute part of the self.

The therapist, through her attunement to her own fluctuant subjective experience while in the inter-subjective dialogue, helps generate relational interactions (herself and patient) that gradually reduce anxiety over recognition by the patient of these warded-off aspects of self. This process in the therapy remains largely implicit and sub-textual, but nevertheless active, largely due to the fluent activity of the therapist's suitably subordinated subjectivity.

11.

Psychotherapy, Adult Development, and the Loving Self

Psychoanalysis is a beneficial experience for its subjects; it is as yet incompletely understood; and it can be perceived from varied perspectives. One such viewpoint, perhaps insufficiently emphasized, is that of adult development. Freud, by introducing the "talking cure," was implicitly endorsing the real possibility of adult development. While much of therapy's manifest content addresses past, early life issues, the process itself is occurring now. The expectation is that the adult life of the subject will improve, i.e. the person will grow.

Yet the facts of therapy arise largely from the revision of deeply ingrained patterns of social living that result from the basic relational circumstances of early life. The success or failure of therapy depends on how well these early relational patterns become understood and revised (where revision is needed).

So, psychotherapy can be regarded as a specific method of promoting adult development. There is special emphasis on the consequences and the origins of childhood-derived patterns of living that extend into the present. These extensions inevitably play an important part in how the person participates in opportunities for adult development, or conversely, copes with obstacles to growth.

Martha Nussbaum, in her book, *Creating Capabilities*, emphasizes that the best approach to optimal adult development is multidimensional. She specifically mentions psychoanalysis as a pertinent resource, not only for understanding the problems and possibilities of adult development, but also as an instrumental form of intervention. Nussbaum writes:

"Considering the various areas of human life in which people move and act, this approach to social justice asks, What does a life worthy of human dignity require? At a bare minimum, an ample threshold level of ten Central Capabilities is required. Given a widely shared understanding of the task of government (namely, that government has the job of making people able to pursue a dignified and minimally flourishing life), it follows that a decent political order must secure to all citizens at least a threshold level of these ten Central Capabilities. (pp. 32-34)

1. Life

2. Bodily health

3. Bodily Integrity

4. Senses, imagination, and thought

5. Emotions

6. Practical reason

7. Affiliation

8. Other species

9. Play

10. Control over one's environment

    A. Political

    B. Material

"Capabilities belong first and foremost to individual persons, and only derivatively to groups. The approach espouses a principle of each person as an end." (p.35)

Nussbaum's ten "central capabilities" correlate well with my insistence that the loving self is triadic: loves itself, loves others, and is loved by others. The correlation exists in that the individual wants, expects, and strives to achieve the ten capabilities; wants, expects, and strives to enable others to achieve these capabilities; and wants, expects, and strives to have others help him or her to achieve these capabilities.

The Psychosocial Loving Self

Thus, we can neatly superimpose the psychosocial conditions necessary for the achievement of capabilities on the essential relational features of the loving self. In turn, this fit reinforces the notion that the loving self is definitely a psychosocial self, rather than just psychological.

As an analytic therapist, my interest and verbal activity are focused on the inhibiting influence of early relational experience upon adult relational fulfillment or lack thereof. Although I am reasonably sophisticated about sociological, economic, and political influences upon quality of life, for individuals as well as groups, I nevertheless do not consciously take immediate account of how these larger forces are operating in the dyadic encounter we call psychotherapy. As a general policy, therapists should pay more attention to the currently prevailing communal values and should think about, or at least sense, how these are significant background—and sometimes foreground—elements in the therapeutic process.

Every one of Nussbaum's ten capabilities concerns the individual's recognition of the legitimacy of her desires/needs. They also represent society's love for personal rights, individual competence, and a voice that will be heard. It seems that the immersion of both patient and therapist in such an environment would constitute a message-laden experience for the two parties. Society is saying: "Both of you are lovable—and loving; you are entitled to recognition, respect, esteem. One of you (patient) is in relatively greater momentary need, but the waters of societal love bathe each of you, promoting the end of fulfilling capabilities in you both."

The patient and therapist are dealing with the vicissitudes of love, as exemplified in the manifold details of the patient's present and early experience, which can only happen as the therapist's successes and failures in a loving life are actively engaged. An atmosphere of social indifference, opposition, or persecution of such human experience would generate anxiety and despair, and, in such a way, would deter—or even destroy—the therapeutic process. Conversely, a society that consistently generates and promotes loving social experience, a la Nussbaum, will reliably and pervasively produce positive reinforcement in the dyadic intimacy of therapy.

Ordinarily, we think about love as a phenomenon occurring between two persons, or at most among a small group, while in larger groups love does not prevail, since the experience of intimacy is diluted and lost amid greater numbers, as is the personal sense of caring about others. Instead, a more impersonal concern is supposed to predominate, based on compassion, fairness, and enlightened self-interest.

Radical Inter-Subjectivity

There is an alternative possibility. Radical inter-subjectivity presumes a certain seamlessness of subjectivity in the human universe. Consider the work of Alfred Schutz, whose revolutionary proposal was that all humans, from the earliest to the ultimate stages of our species, are inter-subjectively engaged. Therefore, if we assume that love is an inter-subjective phenomenon (as described elsewhere in these pages), then it seems valid to assume that love operates between individuals and among group members at all levels of simplicity and complexity—Kant's and the work of other moral thinkers notwithstanding.

On this basis, we should acknowledge that larger group size introduces complicating variables not present in dyadic love relations. However, elements of love are active and present (if often obscurely) in all human engagements, from the most basic to the most complex.

In the above points, I am attempting to establish that psychotherapy is a special form of the general psychosocial process and that however invisibly, social forces are always at work in the therapeutic process.

Let us consider the role of the loving social spirit in the therapeutic process. Love is the primary binding force in human relationships from dyad to family, to clan, to increasingly large communities; and of course, this love may be twisted and obscured in endless ways. We may further assume that societies based on rights, justice, and equality (i.e., societies in which fulfillment of human capabilities is the main goal of social processes), can be considered optimal loving societies.

Individual love powers the dyadic psychotherapeutic relationship, while the societal love in which the therapy is immersed and to which it is responding also contributes constructively to the liberation of love and the loving self. In predominately loving societies, patient and therapist are at least intuitively aware that their joint effort to liberate the loving self enjoys unconditional societal support as a tiny but indispensable element in constructing a society of love.

In the emancipated society, love pervades, in fact undergirds, experience, from the most intimate to the most massive and complex. Therefore, all relational components, small and large, encourage and support all the other loving interactions. And remember, these are all parts of a whole—the seamlessness of human subjectivity and inter-subjectivity!

Such a seamlessly inter-subjective human world presents the optimal condition for psychotherapy. Psychotherapy loses the stain of interiorism, of "self-centeredness." It becomes socially relevant, a significant element in the achievement of social justice and the optimal development of human capabilities. Social fulfillment and individual fulfillment, social love and individual love, cannot ultimately be separable. Social inequities, with short-term advantages for some, ultimately produce net loss of loving experience for one and all.

This indivisibility of love at all levels of human engagement has its justification in the previously mentioned radical inter-subjective concept of the universal, seamless bonding of all humans to one another. The Hegelian notion of the basic nature of love in the dyad can be extrapolated to all other relational configurations. Intensity varies, but not basic quality. This becomes the basis for refuting the notion that morality (distinct from love) creates caring nature in large group relations, while love governs only intimate relationships. This is a false separation of loving and moral attitudes.

Love and Morality

The traditional misconception that love belongs only to the intimate sphere, while morality exists solely in the social zone is based on a concretized and objectified idea of love and morality. The terms should probably be regarded as synonyms with differing connotations: one (love) addressing intimate life, while the other (morality) addresses social life. And there is a quantitative dimension: love's intensity arises in intimacy; morality's passion engages the human community. Love and morality are words about human beings caring for one another: they describe different surfaces of inter-subjective human life.

In blurring the distinctions between love and morality, I am trying to justify the assumption that the social-political climate has continuous interacting relation with each and every person, including the two people in the psychotherapeutic dyad. Psychotherapy that occurs in a society that practices human development a la Nussbaum will be engaging human values that reinforce the loving liberation inherent in the therapeutic relationship.

Perhaps the loving self can only exist, optimally developed, in an advanced society—advanced materially, equitably, and caringly. If indeed love and morality are different manifestations of the same underlying benign inter-subjective passions and intentions and processes, then we can assume social morality and individual loving cannot validly be separated.

The DNA of the Loving Self

In psychotherapy, we experience the loving self visually, audibly, and palpably. We continuously feel the ebb and flow of loving intensity and quality. These immediate impingements tempt us to neglect or disregard the invisible involvements of the loving self. Yet, the loving self extends into communal life, and vice versa. The social values and practices pervade the family life into which the child is born. The parents embody these values and practices.

In this way, the communal qualities suffuse the overt and covert parental attitudes and practices in the intimate parent-child relationships. This seems so obvious, yet its important corollary—the loving self as essentially psychosocial—may be less apparent.

It seems fair to assume that the current rightward drift in the United States is having corrosive effects on the loving self. For example, the neglect of public education represents a contraction of social love, resulting in a reduction of individual and collective literate consciousness. Economic well-being, creativity, political effectiveness, and loving personal relationships all suffer—and each of these losses has some significant negative relation to the loving self.

12.

Supervision and the Loving Self

Supervision occupies a well-deserved, honored position in the field of psychotherapy. It is an intimate and necessary adjunct of psychotherapy and plays an essential role in the training of psychotherapists. Just as psychotherapy is a loving process, so supervision also has the same basis. While psychotherapy is a dyadic experience—therapist and patient, supervision is triadic—patient, therapist (supervisee), and supervisor. Nonetheless, both therapy and supervision provide growth and fulfillment through the underlying force of love.

The nucleus of supervision is the vis-à-vis encounter of the therapist (supervisee) and supervisor, but the conversation concentrates on a third party: the patient. The dialogue is actually—and ostensibly—about the patient, but it is also actually—and ostensibly—about the supervisee, who is busy soaking up therapeutic skill and wisdom. In the meantime, the supervisor is enjoying an infusion of loving energy from the supervisee, whose engagement with the supervisor is reinforced by the relational influence of the patient.

Focusing on the supreme importance of the loving self provides a cohering perspective. The therapist's confidence that the patient is potentially and ultimately a loving person becomes profoundly reassuring to the confused and frightened patient. Therapy then becomes joyous— even with painful disclosures and discomfiting self-discoveries. In this way, belief in the loving self provides a readily graspable basic orientation. A similar, loving belief in the therapist's ability to help the patient provides a cohering perspective for the supervisor-supervisee relationship.

If we agree that loving is recognizing the sentience and neediness of the other, as well as one's own sentient and needy qualities in the other, then we can support the claim that supervision is a specialized form of love, i.e. a lovingly interpretive and identifying focus on a third person who is physically absent from the dialogue. The supervisor is giving love to two persons, and he is receiving love from two. Perhaps we may infer that in terms of relational intensity, the supervisory experience carries exceptional relational force.

Receiving and providing recognition occurs with especial power in certain dyadic relationships—psychotherapy is one. The primary aim of supervision is the enhancement of therapeutic power. As I have emphasized elsewhere, psychotherapy is a specialized loving process, and it follows inexorably that effective supervision must also be a loving experience.

In effect, when the supervisor listens or talks, his honest spontaneity is a continuous necessity, yet he must, at least intuitively, have some understanding of the separate, but commingled needs and offerings of both patient and supervisee. Further complicating is the fact that the patient's presence is mediated entirely through the supervisee.

Again, the fundamental value of psychotherapy is the mobilization and liberation of the loving self. The same is true of the basic effect of supervision. The origin of the loving self lies in the earliest and subsequent family experiences in each and every person. Since psychotherapy liberates the loving self, inevitably family issues are relived and transformed in the therapeutic experience. If supervision is to promote growth for the therapist and stimulate the therapeutic process, it must also partake of the family process that determines therapeutic interaction.

Parenthetically, this emphasis on the intersubjective complexity does not divert the supervisor from serious, conscious attention to evidence of therapeutic progress, such as symptom reduction, energic and affective developments, and relational achievements. Unsurprisingly, the supervisor's immersion in the complex triadic intimacy enriches the supervisor's appreciation of the complex clinical phenomena that require recognition and discussion with the supervisee.

When we employ the family model of supervisory interaction, we see that the neophyte supervisee relates as child to parent (supervisor). In contrast, more experienced supervisees experience the supervisor as sibling. Dominancy, submission, assertiveness, dependency, mastery, competitiveness, fearfulness, playfulness, and other pertinent experiential qualities will vary according to the parent/sibling ratio that exists between the supervisor and the supervisee.

How It Works

Every supervisor (every therapist) develops a theory, a concept that guides his or her practice. My own preference is the theory of the loving self: We thrive as humans through love; it is the basis of our development. Psychotherapy is a loving process that nurtures and liberates the loving self. This theory guides my work as a therapist and as a supervisor. The deceptive simplicity of this theory enables the unfolding of the complexity of the unique configuration of the inner life of the patient. Focus on the loving self encourages activation and exploration of the inevitable presence of unmetabolized aggression in the patient.

When I meet a new supervisee, I make an early estimate of the functioning of her loving self and how it will help to shape our nascent relationship. I consider this an essential step. As our dialogue moves forward, I am mindful of our loving interaction and its usefulness in the supervisee's developmental progress. I do not consider this attitude to be a covert form of therapy; I am more interested in helping the supervisee achieve functional familiarity with the importance of the loving self.

The supervisor finds many opportunities to point out to the supervisee instances of defective (or absent) functioning of the patient's loving self and how this distortion of the optimal influences the therapeutic dialogue. This helps the supervisee to recognize the dysfunctional activity of anger, anxiety, guilt, shame, or other dysphoric elements in the patient's personal life, as well as in the therapeutic relationship.

By maintaining focus on the loving self, the supervisor provides the supervisee with a clear sense of purpose and direction. At the same time, the supervisee enjoys more freedom to attend to the endless and ongoing diversity of the therapeutic events, all the while maintaining a steady sense of the loving self emerging (slowly or rapidly). An otherwise bewildering sense of cacophonous stimuli can thus be taken in and organized around the primary focus: the optimal emancipation of the loving self.

This perspective can be useful even when the supervisee prefers a different theory of therapy. The loving self is not a dogmatic theory, demanding slavish devotion and repudiation of all other theories! I find that Freudian, Kleinian-Bionian, Kohutian, and other theories can be included in an approach that accords centrality to the loving self. Use of multiple theoretical positions while maintaining attention to the loving self enlivens rather than vitiates the therapeutic experience.

As supervisor, I view the supervisory process as another form of loving interaction—with a defining emphasis on development of the supervisee's therapeutic skills. With this attitude, I strive to identify with the supervisee and to develop interpretive possibilities for the supervisee's consideration in working with the patient.

Two Caveats

The effect of supervision results from a loving process involving supervisor and supervisee—with two provisos. One is that the emphasis of the process is on change in the therapist that enhances his love-based interactive and interventional skills on behalf of the patient. The second is that the change in the therapist is achieved through dialogue that manifestly is about the patient, not the therapist. Although supervisory discussion often includes the therapist's conflicts, anxieties, resistances, and countertransferences, such discussion is mutually understood to be primarily in service of helping the therapist to help the patient.

So, to order priorities: the supervisory dialogue concentrates primarily on the patient; secondarily on the therapist; and thirdly on the presumably more mature supervisor, whose loving engagement to his or her own self and to the human world is relatively advanced and conscious.

The supervisee is the centerpiece of supervision. After all, it is the supervisee (the therapist) who links patient and supervisor, creating the triadic intersubjective bridge.

As the therapist interacts with the supervisor, the therapist's inner life carries her process with the patient. The supervisor responds to the patient, whose psychological presence is brought by the therapist. A sophisticated supervisor realizes that he is influencing and being influenced by the therapist directly and by the patient indirectly. But the hapless patient is usually unaware of the influential third party (the supervisor).

The Initial Phase of Supervision

In the beginning of the supervisory process, the ingénue is typically frightened. She often feels lacking in skill and seeks instruction. A supervisor should be generous in this period with specifics regarding interventions: how to listen, question, suggest, answer the patient's questions, and other basic skills. From the beginning a supervisor offers himself for modeling by the inexperienced, often intimidated supervisee.

The supervisor's understanding—not patronizing—attitude will help the supervisee to optimize her own empathic skills. The supervisor also teaches by example: using key dialogic strategies with the supervisee, such as: reading between the lines, inference—low level to high level, and sensitive "guessing."

The supervisor identifies primarily with the supervisee, but also with the patient. In this way, the supervisor can be in touch with the basic relational experience of the therapeutic pair. This relationship undergirds the entire therapeutic process—beginning to end—and should be a continuing focus of the supervisor.

Formulation by the supervisor should be achieved rapidly, but also flexibly. Rapidly, to give the supervisee a sense of coherence and security if he or she is floundering in inexperience, but flexibly enough to be revised if the initial formulation is seriously in error or fragmentary and incomplete.

The supervisor must convey confidence in the supervisee's ability. This is where focusing on the patient's feelings and intuiting the patient's relational issues are very helpful. The patient, after all, expects and receives something from the therapist. The supervisor can help the therapist to appreciate this fact, especially at the outset but throughout supervision as well. By aiding the therapist (supervisee) realize she is already helping the patient at the early stage of therapy, the supervisor provides essential support.

In this initial phase, it is very important that the supervisor and the trainee are well matched by a coordinator who knows enough about both the trainee and the supervisor to increase the possibility that the two will work well together.

A beginning supervisee will always be anxiously hopeful for a supervisory experience that will generate appropriate confidence in the therapeutic process. From the outset, the effective supervisor will exude an implicit and often explicit conviction that good work in psychotherapy takes place in the absence of comprehensive clarity as to the meanings of the patient's major symptoms, behaviors, and relational difficulties. The message must be clear: the supervisee can gradually bring ultimate order out of initial chaos.

The supervisor should greet the new supervisee with warmth, respect, and appreciation for the high probability that the supervisee is frightened and intimidated. The supervisor might say, "I realize how overwhelmed you are, but it is always that way in the beginning. It's actually a welcome sign that you are strongly motivated to be helpful to your patient. As we navigate the rocks and shoals of this opening phase, your comfort and confidence, not complacency, will rapidly grow." (Here, the supervisor should realize and welcome the fact that the supervisee is voraciously identifying with the supervisor.)

Initially, I invite the supervisee to tell me about the patient. I ask why the patient has come to therapy, and how—reluctantly, eagerly, through family, friends, courts? What is the current problem? What is the individual's history? What is the diagnosis from previous therapy?

As indicated above, early formulation by the supervisor reassures the therapist that, in the vast disorganized sprawl of the patient's presentation, it is quite possible to discover and articulate crucial foci of meaning in the patient's life, by attending to one's own inner responses to the patient's therapeutic behavior (verbal and nonverbal). The supervisee may well then feel that if the supervisor can make these illuminating inferences, then she also can achieve this skill. The therapist will take this new capability back to her meetings with the patient and she will enjoy heightened interest in her own ongoing thoughts and feelings, realizing their potential value in reading between the patient's lines. This is a loving process. It is a major step in the therapist's ability to develop a skill in free associative listening that enables therapeutic identification with the patient.

Early in the supervisory dialogue I invite the supervisee to open our session with a brief summary of her session or sessions with the patient since our last meeting. This provides an overview (without details) of the current therapy and has special value when the therapy occurs multiple times per week, rather than weekly or every other week. Even for less intensive therapy, this practice has value, since it encourages and enables the therapist to make an active thinking and feeling investment of self in the therapy session, through which the supervisee can perceive this therapy session as a semiautonomous entity with unique meaning, within a larger process composed of an ongoing sequence of interrelated entities. In his summarizing activity, the supervisor is promoting panoramic vistas coexisting with finely tuned focal attention to the session and its assemblage of specific meanings.

Support and Early Formulation

The typical supervisee has a conceptual background in therapy but very little experience of practical therapy. A trainee who has been in therapy is fortunate indeed, because a genuine immersion in therapy certainly provides experience of therapeutic ambience, thinking, interventions, etc., all of which increase sensitivity to supervision.

I have polled about a dozen therapists who are now or have been my supervisees. Uniformly, they cited support as a critical necessity, especially in the early phase of supervision. The perception of common ground and shared enthusiasm for a particular case and for teaching and learning is a kind of loving embrace by the supervisor, who senses the therapist's anxiety. Simultaneously, the supervisor's active interest is intensified by the supervisee's grateful relaxation and the consequent conveyance of the inner richness of her ongoing dialogue with the patient.

A second positive experience cited by those polled is the supervisor's rapid formulation (often as early as the first supervisory session) of the fundamental therapeutic issue confronting the therapist. The presentation by the supervisee includes a complex subtext that is conveyed along with the manifest report. In the loving interplay of supervisor and supervisee, this crucial subtext is occurring and the attuned supervisor derives meaning from these loving offerings to the supervision from the supervisee.

Support and early formulation—both significant elements in a goal-directed loving interaction—become basic to a stable, productive supervisory relationship. This loving relationship becomes a great influence in the proliferation of a truth-seeking therapeutic dialogue with transformative potential. Thus the triadic (therapist, patient, supervisor) relationship grows and gains productive power. The supervisee gains confidence that she can know the patient (i.e. understand and recognize the patient) and grasp the essential conflicts with which the patient struggles. The patient who receives the loving message of confidence and recognition responds to the therapist with loving disclosures of inner meanings that confirm the therapist's intuitively based inferences, thus encouraging the therapist to extend her understanding more deeply and widely, adding more and more power to the productively circular process.

The therapist then brings her ongoing therapeutic dialogue to the supervisor—thus sharing the underlying process of mutual recognition—mostly with emphasis on the patient's changing investment in the therapeutic relationship. The supervisee reveals her accomplishments and her needs to the supervisor. This is a loving infusion by the supervisee, and it invigorates the supervisor's interest in the supervisee. The supervisee is inescapably sharing her own life themes (subtextually) as she advances in formulating the patient's issues. Similarly, the supervisor's responsive participation is partially (but necessarily) shaped by the supervisor's own impinging life theme. In turn, this supervisory input advances the therapist's sense of self. In her further dialogue with the patient, the therapist brings new stimulating meanings derived from her current supervision.

Listen, Feel, Think, Talk

Typically in supervision the supervisor is listening to the speaking voice of the supervisee. This is complex enough, since the supervisee speaks, expecting to hear, in response, keys to facilitating therapy with the patient being presented, and thus also expecting refinement of her technique and an expansion of her therapeutic horizons. In order to derive these benefits, the therapist must also bring the voice of the patient, partially hidden, as an important component of the presentation to the supervisor. Thus the supervisor listens simultaneously to two voices.

I insist that when the supervisor provides new ideas, he is responding to the patient, through the therapist. The supervisor's response contains subtle elements addressing the unconscious needs of the therapist as well. All three are in touch with the patient's pertinent truths: the therapist receives the patient's preliminary hints of meaning; the supervisor listens with his "third ear," and then is able to discern (tentatively) the patient's salient relational conflict. He delivers it back, suitably edited, to the therapist, in a form that harmonizes with the therapist's leading relational issues through which she is giving and receiving communication.

Thus the supervisor has enabled the therapist to achieve the interpretive moment with the patient who is presumably poised to receive this loving input from the therapist.

The therapist's feelings about the patient and the supervisor provide clues as to the patient's underlying relational issues. The supervisor uses his own feelings, which reveal the subordinated subjectivity of the therapist and of the supervisor. They in turn can be used in formulating the unconscious processes with the patient.

The subjective responsiveness of the supervisor to the supervisee does not usually entail a disturbance of the supervisory process. In fact, my experience leads me to believe that such responsiveness is a valuable component of the supervisor's understanding. In one instance, for example, a female supervisee who had been severely rejected by her authoritarian father clearly needed a paternal loving response from me. Her subsequent identification with me enabled her to more confidently assume a parental stance with her similarly deprived patient.

The supervisor's participation includes continuous emotional involvement. These feelings are inseparable from the supervisor's activity. These feelings usually provide useful leads to the prevailing emotions of the patient and therapist. But they are embedded in the supervisor's unique emotional responsiveness. This circumstance provides challenge and opportunity. The supervisor is aware of his own basic subjective issue through which he can infer the crucial subjective element of the patient. Additionally, the supervisor can perceive useful hints of the supervisee's concurrent subjective experience that is carrying and shaping the presenting issue of the patient. To reiterate: optimally, the thoughts and feelings of the supervisor constitute a similar unit of meaning.

Most supervisees insist that a prime benefit of supervision is basic but flexible formulation by the supervisor, provided, as I noted earlier, in an expeditious manner. I try, with fair regularity, to offer a formulation in the initial supervisory meeting. It may be that making an early formulation is even more appropriate and desirable for the supervisor than for the supervisee, who should be immersing herself in the plethora of complaints, concerns, memories, etc. of the patient at the outset. In a way, the therapist protects the supervisor from the patient's clamorous impact, enabling the supervisor to enjoy the luxury of reflective thought. This, in turn, enables the supervisor to give back a coherent sense of order and developmental promise.

This supervisory process has another helpful implication for the therapist's development. The supervisor's demonstrative capacity to stay cool while also involved models a less anxious response for the therapist. This in turn enables the therapist to intervene interpretively and empathically, sooner. All parties in the supervisory triad thus achieve increased liberation of the loving self—the patient being the prime beneficiary.

The Supervisor's Attitude

Supervision is an experience of adult development. The supervisee is a junior colleague in training who optimally regards the supervisor as someone whose thinking and experience have established therapeutic skills that the supervisee wants and needs to develop. This can be achieved through an optimal supervisory dialogue.

This dialogue begins, as I have noted, with a report on the discussion between the patient and the therapist (supervisee). This is followed by a discussion between the supervisor and supervisee on the ongoing progress of therapy. This leads to a discussion of the unconscious (subtextual) process—not only the client's unconscious issues, but also the unconscious intersubjective process. This provides a valuable opportunity to identify the crucial central relational themes of the client and their instructive interaction with the supervisee's salient themes. (In therapy, the patient's subjectivity is dominant; the therapist's is necessary but restrained.)

So, supervision includes the therapist's subjectivity as an important, always active factor; therefore it is an indispensable component of the supervisory dialogue. This should not be thought of as an intermittently occurring countertransference. Instead, the focus is on the supervisee's subjectivity and how it affects the therapeutic process—optimally the therapist's subjectivity is subordinated (see Chapter 6). As the supervisee feels safe and comfortable in supervision, the supervisor should include a discussion of the intersubjective process and it's invaluable role in moving the therapy along.

The above emphases naturally encourage and enable the therapist to achieve appropriate identification with the patient. Appropriate identification permits the therapist to be optimally self-knowing and self-defining. She is not in danger of losing a sense of her separateness and difference and retains her capacity to discern meanings, defenses, etc. In the case of inappropriate identification the therapist identifies excessively with the patient's anxiety, rage, depression, which impairs the therapist's reflective activity.

Later Phases of Supervision

Various Formats for Long-Term Supervision

The theme of early formulation by the supervisor recurs. This need exists with more advanced supervisees as well as neophytes. A significant portion of my supervisory practice involves experienced therapists who meet with me weekly (intensive) or monthly (non-intensive), but with the same specific interest, i.e., to present a new therapy case and to obtain (usually in one session, but not always) a more clear concept of the patient's basic underlying problem (a relational conflict and the consequent disturbance of self-fulfilling engagement with the world).

In such longstanding dyadic supervisory arrangements, the learning needs of the supervisee are much different from those of the inexperienced trainee. In fact, it may be misleading to refer to learning needs in these situations. These seasoned therapists are at ease in their therapeutic role and are not anxiously seeking to learn how to do therapy. They feel confident in their basic skills. They have voluntarily sought supervision and they know, generally, what to expect. These sophisticated supervisees seek a synthesis of contrasts; i.e., how does the therapist see the patient and how does the supervisor see the same patient. Here it is not a case of ignorance seeking knowledge; or error needing correction. The supervisor appreciates that such a supervisee intends to superimpose, to merge the two perspectives, and thereby to achieve a more advanced understanding of the patient and the therapeutic interaction.

A certain level of anxiety should occur in the supervisor with both the beginner and the experienced supervisees. But rescue fantasies are not as intense or frequent when working with experienced therapists. One might consider the unconscious relational fantasy of the supervisor is more one of a suitably anxious parent, who provides a safe and growth-promoting environment for the vulnerable therapeutic ingénue. With experienced therapists, the supervisor may relate more as a sibling with special interests that the supervisee is now also becoming interested in.

The Spirit of the Supervisory Experience

Whatever the relational configuration of the supervisor and supervisee, there is always a shared experience of mutual growth. One recurring theme in the literature on supervision emphasizes the risk of supervision lapsing into therapy for the supervisee. My own extensive experience over many decades informs me that such risk is negligible—even when situations develop during the course of supervision, when we focus for a brief period on a subjective disturbance in the supervisee that is disrupting the therapeutic progress.

Consider this example, in which a brief therapeutic interlude was seamlessly woven into the enlarging fabric of the supervisory experience:

Eric is a middle-aged, experienced psychologist who had been in weekly supervision with me for two years. We developed a productive dialogue, characterized by mutually respectful and trusting feelings. Then, one day, Eric began a session by telling me that he had become extremely anxious during the preceding few days. He said that he understood it in some ways but wanted to talk with me about it, since it seemed to involve his work.

He proceeded to tell me that two weeks earlier he had begun therapy with a new patient. He described her as an angry, loud, self-righteous person who reminded him very much of his mother, evoking in him angry memories from his boyhood, when he felt helplessly abused by his mother, and unprotected by his father. Now he was experiencing intense free-floating anxiety that was damaging his work performance.

As Eric and I spoke, he realized that he was conflating this woman with his mother, and was feeling hatred and then guilt toward her. He reported that he had also felt some angry feelings toward me, fearing that I would send him to someone else for therapy and in that way I would avoid protecting him, in a way similar to his father's neglect.

As Eric returned to his early suffering at his mother's hands, the displacement of the pain to his new patient subsided. He was now able to experience her as a woman who needed his help—not as a replica of his mother. His anxiety rapidly melted away, and we were able to resume our typical supervisory dialogue.

A supervisory climate of mutual trust and friendship is conducive to another quasi-therapeutic condition occurring in some supervisions. This circumstance may occur early or later in supervision. In these cases, the supervisee reveals to the supervisor profoundly traumatic intra-familial events. The stated motive for the revelation is to make the supervisor aware of the supervisee's major internal preoccupation and to be able to include it, where appropriate, in the supervisor's reflective responsiveness within the supervisory dialogue. When such disclosures occur, whatever their deeper meaning to the supervision, they are not for "therapy." The revelations are prompted by the supervisee's wish for the supervisor to be aware of the traumatized filter through which the supervisee experiences the therapeutic interaction, and for the supervisor to have a more comprehensive awareness of the total intersubjective field of the therapy. The joint establishment of safety is the necessary precondition for the supervisee's maturely motivated revelations and their disclosure to the supervisor. Sharing these revelations with the supervisor is often profoundly painful for the supervisee. It is an act of collaborative courage and constructiveness.

Group Supervision

A supervisory group usually consists of four to eight supervisees who meet regularly with a supervisor. Typically, one case is presented by one of the supervisees, and an order of presentation is established so that there is a stable rotation of presenters. Those supervisees who are not presenting in a particular session have an opportunity to function in a somewhat supervisory mode. As in any group, complex group interactions occur to which the supervisor should attend. Otherwise, hostile acting out, clique formation, or other inappropriate modes of participation can undermine the achievement of a constructive and beneficial group ambience and process.

An important gain from group supervision is the presenting supervisee's experience of having multiple constructive critical responses from the various group members. The other group members can also benefit from the multiple perspectives that form the discussion. Any supervisory group will be unified by the shared motivation of the members and by the relational bonds generated by the shared immersion in emotionally charged issues that are the basic sustained focus of the group. Sustained alienation and tendentiously based battles are counter-productive. Yet, shifting feelings of closeness and antagonism, as well as approving or disapproving do occur. These are responses to a presenter's or a commentator's way of understanding theoretical concepts and style of communication with a patient. Such developments can be very instructive and revealing components of the shared experience.

Another potential value of group supervision concerns ethical and legal questions. The multiplicity of opinions about such matters can be very helpful in achieving balanced policy decisions. Although group supervision has similarities to individual supervision, group supervision's numerous unique features render it a qualitatively different experience. Furthermore, group supervision should be a component of a therapist's experience at some point in her educational involvement. Group supervision and group therapy overlap in some ways, although they have basic differences, and so the experience of group supervision can only help the therapist in developing skills for working with groups.

Peer Supervision

The preceding discussion essentially deals with conventional hierarchically-based supervision. But another form of supervision exists, called peer supervision. It is egalitarian and non-hierarchical.

Typically, in peer supervision a number of therapists, ranging between four and ten, meet to discuss cases. Usually, they call this a *study group*. It is leaderless. A regular rotation of presentation exists, and the atmosphere is informal and collegial. New cases, problem cases, and special interest cases are presented.

In such groups, close relationships develop. The loving energy generated in the relational dialogue strengthens the loving selves of the members, which, in turn, enlarges the loving capabilities of the patients whose lives are brought in to the group through the presentations. The wide acceptance of peer group supervision by therapists demonstrates that an authoritarian element is not intrinsic to supervision.

Nurturing the Supervisory Relationship

Recognition, respect, sentience, dignity, capability, vulnerability, trust, self-disclosure, and self-reflection: These nine qualities all have relevance for supervision. The supervisor's achievement of self-recognition and self-respect facilitates the achievement of these qualities by the supervisee, who in turn fosters their development by the patient. The sentience, dignity, capability, and vulnerability of the supervisee are implicitly and explicitly appreciated by the mature supervisor. The therapeutic sensitivity of the supervisee is correspondingly enlarged.

Mutual trust in supervision fosters self-disclosure and ever-increased self-reflection in the supervisee. These qualities will grow in the therapeutic relationship as well. It seems obvious that these experiences in supervision are powerfully conducive to growth of the loving self.

References
(in order of appearance)

Introduction

Natterson, J.M. (2003) Love in psychotherapy. *Psychoanalytic Psychology* 20(3): 509–21.

Phillips, A. & Taylor, B. (2009). *On Kindness*. New York: Farrar, Straus and Giroux.

Rifkin, J. (2009). *The Empathic Civilization: The Race to Global Consciousness in a World in Crisis*. New York: J.P. Tarcher/Penguin.

Chapter Two

Lear, J. (1990). *Love and Its Place in Nature: A Philosophical Interpretation of Freudian Psychoanalysis*. New York: Farrar, Straus & Giroux.

Gaylin, W. & Person, E.S. (1988). *Passionate Attachments: Thinking about Love*. New York: Free Press.

Freud, S. (1920). *A General Introduction to Psychoanalysis.* New York: Boni and Liveright,

Honneth, A. (1996). *The Struggle for Recognition: The Moral Grammar of Social Conflicts - Kampf Um Anerkennung. English.* Trans. Joel Anderson. MIT Press.

Hegel, G.W., Harris, H.S. & Knox, T.M. (1979). *System of Ethical Life (1802/3) and First Philosophy of Spirit (part III of the System of Speculative Philosophy 1803/4)*. Albany: State University of New York.

Bourdieu, P. (2000). *Pascalian Meditations*. Stanford, CA: Stanford University Press.

Freud, S. *Ibid.*

Ferenczi, S. & Dupont. J. (1988). *The Clinical Diary of Sándor Ferenczi.* Cambridge, MA: Harvard University Press.

Alexander, F. & French, T.M. (1946). *Psychoanalytic Therapy; Principles and Application.* New York: Ronald.

Reik, T. (1948). *Listening with the Third Ear; the Inner Experience of a Psychoanalyst.* New York: Farrar, Straus.

Greenson, R.R. (1965). The working alliance and the transference neurosis. *Psychoanalytic Quarterly* 34:155–81.

Racker, H. (1968). *Transference and Counter-transference.* New York: International Universities Press.

Kohut, H. (1977). *The Restoration of the Self.* New York: International Universities Press.

Chapter Three

Hegel, G.W.F. *Ibid.*

Honneth, A. *Ibid.*

Winnicott, D. W. "The Use of an Object and Relating through Identification." *The Maturational Processes and the Facilitating Environment; Studies in the Theory of Emotional Development.* London: Hogarth, 1965. 86–94.

Loewald, H.W. *Papers on Psychoanalysis.* New Haven: Yale UP, 1980.

Loewald, H.W. *Ibid.*

Machiavelli, N. (2009). *The Prince.* Trans. Tim Parks. New York: Penguin.

Hobbes, T. (1991). *Leviathan.* Cambridge, England: Cambridge University Press.

Skolnick, N.J., & Warshaw, S.C.. "Recognition and Destruction: An Outline of Intersubjectivity." *Relational Perspectives in Psychoanalysis*. Hillsdale, NJ: Analytic, 1992. 43–60.

Honneth, A. (2008). *Reification: A New Look at an Old Idea*. Oxford: Oxford University Press.

Butler, J. (2008). Taking Another's View: Ambivalent Implications in *Reification: A New Look at an Old Idea*. Oxford: Oxford University Press, 97–120.

Lear, J. (2008). The Slippery Middle om *Reification: A New Look at an Old Idea*. Oxford: Oxford University Press, 131–147.

Freud, S. *Ibid.*

Grotjahn, Mn. *Beyond Laughter; Humor and the Subconscious.* New York: McGraw-Hill, 1966.

Alexander, F. & French, T. *Ibid.*

Sartre, J.-P. (1990). *Being and Nothingness.* Routledge,

Foucault, M. (1975.). *Discipline and Punish: The Birth of Prison*. Trans. Alan Sheridan. London: Penguin.

Derrida, J. (1998). *Resistances of Psychoanalysis*. Stanford, CA: Stanford University Press.

Winnicott, D.W. *Ibid.*

Rifkin, J. *Ibid.*

Taylor, B. *Ibid.*

Phillips, A. *Ibid.*

Freud, S. *Ibid.*

Gadamer, H. (1975). *Truth and Method*. New York: Seabury.

Honneth, Axel. *Ibid.*

Boston Process Change Study Group, comp. (2010). *Change in Psycho-therapy: A Unifying Paradigm*. New York: W.W. Norton & Co,.

Gadamer, H.-G. *Ibid.*

Loewald, H.W. *Ibid.*

Bourdieu, P. *Ibid.*

Freud, S. *Ibid.*

Auden, W. H. (1991). *Collected Poems*. Ed. Edward Mendelson. New York: Vintage International, Vintage.

Hopkins, G.M. & Bridges, R. (1918). *Poems of Gerard Manley Hopkins*. London: Humphrey Milford.

Nussbaum, M.C. (2011). *Creating Capabilities: The Human Develop-ment Approach*. Cambridge, MA: Belknap of Harvard University Press.

Schutz, A. (1967). *The Phenomenology of the Social World.* [Evanston, Ill.]: Northwestern University Press.